THE WORST OF GOLF

Dale Concannon

Shanks to slip ups: Malice and missed putts in the world's most frustrating game

1

Dale Concannon is a full-time golf journalist and author of 14 books on the game. A former PGA professional, he is a regular contributor to many international publications and is the author of the Sunday Times bestselling biography of Nick Faldo, *Driven*. Among his previous books are *Golf: The Early Days, From Tee to Green, The Round of My Life* and *The Ryder Cup: Seven Decades of Golfing Glory, Passion and Controversy*. He is also the owner of the Concannon Golf History Photography Collection and a member of the Golf World panel that selects the top-100 British Golf Courses.

THE WORST OF GOLF

Dale Concannon

Shanks to slip ups: Malice and misfortune in the world's most frustrating game

The Worst of Golf
Shanks to Slip Ups: Malice and Missed Putts in the World's Most Frustrating Game

© 2005, 2008 Dale Concannon

Publishing by:

Pitch Publishing (Brighton) Ltd
A2 Yeoman Gate
Yeoman Way
Worthing BN13 3QZ
Email: info@pitchpublishing.co.uk
Web: www.pitchpublishing.co.uk

First published 2005.

ISBN 978-1905411191 2ND EDITION
(ISBN 978-0954246082 FIRST EDITION)

Picture credits:

Empics: Pages; 13, 47.

Phil Sheldon Golf Picture Library: 29, 61, 97, 141, 169.

Dale Concannon Golf Picture Library: 77, 113, 127, 153.

Illustrations by: Luke Jefford & Elaine Shields

Editor: Roy Chuter

Cover and page design:

Luke Jefford & Associates
Tel: 01273 297 872
Email: luke@lukejefford.com

Printed and bound in Great Britain by The Cromwell Press

Contents

Foreword by Mark Roe

Friends often tell me that I have the best job in the world.

"Look at you," they say, "swanning around the world enjoying yourself." Then, as if the words Income Tax, hotel bills and caddie fees had never been invented, they rabbit on about some rose-tinted Utopia where I spend my waking hours "rubbing shoulders with the rich and famous and earning a fortune just for hitting a golf ball around a field."

Even the legendary entrepreneur Mark McCormack thought I had it cracked, as he believed the secret of a happy life was "to find a job you would do for nothing, then get paid for it!"

He was probably right, and only a fool would argue that playing golf for a living is not a pleasant way to turn a bob or two. Yet it does have its drawbacks, not least of which is the fact that we are never off duty.

For example, when a council worker pops down his local to unwind after a day's hard toil, he is fairly certain that no-one will approach him, writ in hand, demanding to know why a bypass is going to pass through his back garden! These matters are work-related, and therefore reserved for normal business hours. Even doctors, who used to be considered fair game for anyone with a dodgy back or swollen extremities, are now left in blissful silence… but not pro golfers – and especially not someone who is often seen playing tournaments on the box.

Considered fair game by anyone who has ever picked up a club, they zero in on you like their life depended on it. "Hello," will say a friendly voice. "I expect you've been at the golf. I saw the highlights last night. Tell me, is it true that Tiger is successful because his right arm is two inches longer than his left? I read somewhere that is why he is so good."

Waving over his mate from the other side of the room, the entire pub is now awaiting an exclusive insight which inevitably ends in crushing disappointment when you admit that, far from being Mr Woods' best mate, you have never actually met him, socially or otherwise.

"What a life you chaps have," he continues, undeterred. "Still, I expect you will want to get back and watch the highlights at 11.45. You won't want to miss those, will you? By the way, will you take a look at my grip, I am slicing it a bit at the moment."

The splintering sound that may be heard at this point is the hapless pro biting chunks out of his glass as he finds himself holding hands with a hitherto perfect stranger in the middle of a bar!

Of course this is not always the case. Sometimes when you tell someone what you do, the reaction is often a loud belly laugh, followed by a quizzical look, then a comment along the lines of: "No, really, what do you *really* do?"

The trouble is that, for most people, golf is a pleasurable pastime totally removed from their own job of work. For others it can be a real obsession, which brings me to the subject matter of this excellent book by Dale Concannon.

For as long as I have known him, he has collected wonderfully bizarre stories from the sport's historic past, and reading through the pages, I really start to wonder how crazy you have to be to play golf in the first place. I also note that some of the stories involve my fellow tournament players (me included!), which shows how golf affects us all to varying degrees. Would I have done things differently given the opportunity? You bet your life I would, which incidentally is what I read two golfers did in St Andrews over a century ago!

Rabbit or tiger, hacker or pro, I am sure you will enjoy The Worst of Golf as much as I did.

MARK ROE
European Tour Professional:
1989 Catalan Open winner,
1992 Lancôme Trophy winner,
and 1994 French Open winner.

Introduction

Ever wondered why you play golf?" That was the question put to me by an eminent psychologist who was obviously looking for extra customers from among the ranks of the golfing media.

"Because I enjoy it?" came my somewhat faltering reply. "Ah, but do you really?" he said fixing me with that quizzical stare all trick cyclists save for their most interesting cases.

We had just spent five hours in each other's company at a corporate golf day and perhaps I was not performing at my peak. My game was a little off and yes, I may have said a few things about the condition of the greens, my clubs, my driving, my inability to concentrate for more than two shots in a row… And yes, the odd Anglo-Saxonism may have passed my lips after a card-wrecking triple-bogey on the par-three seventh but nothing he could possibly misconstrue as me not enjoying it…

Not that his golf game was that impressive. He played in that happy, flappy, only-took-the-game-up-last-week way that infuriates all serious golfers. He was courteous and polite and never failed to say "bad luck" as my tee-shots found more trees than Robin Hood's Merry Men!

If only it had ended there. Halfway through he pulled me over for an impromptu-putting lesson and like all new-born golfers he was a crashing rules bore: "No you cannot drop it there," he told me on the fifteenth in his best "I-feel-your-pain" voice. "Your only option is to go all the way back to the tee…"

I realised later it was not my only option. I could have throttled him with his newly purchased 'Tiger' head cover and left the course to the scream of police sirens a very happy man. That said, it did not answer the fundamental question about what it was I actually enjoyed about golf? After all, I had been playing the damn silly game for the best part of three decades and something must have pulled me toward it.

Grabbing a pen, I decided to list what I liked about golf and it proved quite revealing. Top of the list was the fresh air and exercise…

Reality, however, was a little different. After the briefest amount of soul – searching I came to the conclusion that I considered fresh air in terms of how far the wind would divert my ball off line and whether the cold temperature would affect the compression of the ball! As for exercise, that also proved a pure fantasy as I am always the first to demand an electric buggy whether the course is hard walking or not!

What about meeting new people, I pondered. In truth, the older I get the less I want to play with strangers with their incessant chatter and quirky personal habits, so that proved a dead end. And what about those solitary trips to the practice ground where pounding golf balls made me feel closer to nature? That brought on a warm fuzzy feeling but it soon dissipated after I could not remember where it was located since my home Club moved it ten years ago…

This set me thinking. To play golf is the search for perfection – a seemingly endless struggle to hit 300-yard power fades, pin-splitting irons and pressure – defying putts. It requires a complete mastery over emotion, nerve and temper with success or failure depending on the individuals' ability to handle all three at once. After all, in what other game are you expected to summon up the ability to drive a stationary ball with the force of a sledge-hammer one moment, then chip it with the delicate touch of a heart surgeon the next? I reasoned that no other game offered so much potential for failure and such little reward for success.

So was it any wonder that I did not enjoy the game? As an average golfer, I am always going to hit more bad shots than good, miss more putts than I hole and fluff more chips than I hole out. In short the odds are stacked against me before I even start. So why do I carry on? The answer is simple. Because every time I step onto that first tee I expect to play well. Like those deluded people who believe in Santa Claus, alien abductions and non-self-serving politicians, I truly hope that this will be the day that I exceed all my expectations. Has it ever happened? Well, I still live in hope.

Which brings me neatly to *The Worst of Golf*. As fellow devotees you will be shocked by many of the stories but surprised by none. You will shake your head and wonder just how people could get themselves into such a state. Then you rush straight out for nine holes and you know exactly why.

As many of these wonderfully quirky stories reveal, golf is a hugely frustrating sport played by people who really should know better. I had a lot of fun putting it together and I hope you have just as much fun reading it.

Play great golf!

Dale Concannon

CHAPTER ONE

The worst behaved golfers ever

The worst-behaved golfers ever

Golf is a game for gentlemen – or so we are led to believe. **In keeping with this Corinthian** ideal, the British public expected its heroes not only to win tournaments, but to win them in style, with little more than a modest wave of the hand here, a tip of the hat there. But did they? Well…

Today, things are different. Like many other sports in this television-driven world, the way professionals conduct themselves on and off the golf course has changed enormously over the past century. In the early 1900s, they were little more than servants who mended clubs, gave the odd lesson and caddied for the idle rich.

Three decades later, even superstar players like Harry Vardon retained a club position to maintain a half-decent standard of living, and as recently as the 1960s, the vast majority of British professionals were not allowed in the clubhouse in case it upset the members!

Today, with the final stages of many golf tournaments televised worldwide, the result often hinges on one moment of brilliance or disaster. With pressure at its absolute height, these are inevitably drama-filled and emotionally-charged occasions. The rewards for success are simply enormous – but so is the pressure, and occasionally things have a way of boiling over.

As many amateur golfers will gladly testify, golf is already the most frustrating game ever invented, and as this chapter reveals, it has a way of getting to us all in the end.

1

Happy Hacker
Maurice Flitcroft
1976 British Open

Written large in Open folklore is Maurice Flitcroft, a 46-year old crane driver from Barrow-in-Furness, who decided to enter the qualifying rounds for the 1976 Championship fully convinced that golf's greatest prize was well within his grasp... the only problem being that he had never played a full 18 holes in his life, and had only taken up playing the game of golf sixteen months earlier.

Not surprisingly, he took 121 strokes, and was immediately disqualified, while the £30 entry fee was refunded to his two furious playing partners.

With the Royal & Ancient Golf Club forced to tighten up entry procedures, further attempts from Flitcroft – under the nom-de-plumes of Gerard Hoppy and Beau Jolley – to enter the British Open were unearthed over the next few years.

2  Norman Conquests
Moe Norman

Moe Norman lived like a tramp, never owned a phone and drank 15 cans of cola a day, but he was considered by Ben Hogan and Sam Snead to be the finest ball-striker they had ever seen. He won 13 events in the 1960s and was reputedly able to recall the yardage of almost every hole he had ever played.

Despite induction into the Canadian Hall of Fame in 1995, it is still Norman's idiosyncrasies that bring him to mind; coming to the final hole with a two-shot lead, for instance, he asked his caddie how he should play it. "A drive followed by a seven-iron, boss," came the reply.

Moe, though, picked out the seven-iron first, and proceeded to hit the ball off the tee! Then, from way back down the fairway, he took his driver out and smashed the ball straight into the heart of the green.

Two putts later he was the champion. "I guess you were right," he said to the shell-shocked caddie.

By 1980, Norman was sleeping rough on park benches and in parked cars. When the boss of a major golf company heard of his plight, he decided to pay Norman a monthly allowance of $5,000.

17

3

Grip it and Rip it
John Daly

John "Wild Thang" Daly had always been as unconventional as he is powerful. In one of the most unexpected victories in major championship history, the flaxen-haired 24-year-old from Arkansas arrived at Crooked Stick, Indiana for the 1991 US PGA having driven hundreds of miles through the night from Memphis. Ninth reserve at the start of the week, he came in as a late replacement for past champion Nick Price who was forced to pull out through injury. More used to socialising with Jack Daniels than Jack Nicklaus, his simple motto of "Grip it and rip it" summed him up perfectly as he romped to victory as a 500–1 outsider.

Mostly self-taught, he learnt the game from watching golf videos as a youngster. Picking up his first golf club at the age of five, his early years were spent annoying the neighbours.

"I used to wade into the ponds on a little nine-hole country club that I grew up on. I wasn't old enough to play on it but I used to take the balls I found onto the baseball field and there was this little guy who I used to fight all the time when I was four or five years old. He lived just across the neighbourhood so I used to take the balls and try and hit his house with them... When I got to about six or seven I started to hit the windows. I was a little bigger than he was but his dad was a lot bigger so I quit."

Having drunk his first beer at eight, he quickly developed a reputation of living life to the full. In between a number of well-publicised divorce cases, high-stakes gambling and bouts of binge drinking that left him visibly shaking on the golf course, he still managed to win the British Open at St Andrews after a play-off with Italian Constantino Rocca in 1995. Known for his big hitting, Daly arrived on the practice ground at Muirfield during the 1992 British Open to find it was not long enough. Despite having a 20-foot high fence erected at a distance of 280 yards, he thrilled the crowds by smashing drive after drive into the rough beyond, much to the annoyance of the organisers. Not surprisingly, the Championship committee took the decision to move the fence back in the interests of public safety. Still a huge draw wherever he plays, his story remains one of the best rags-to-riches tales in the world of sport.

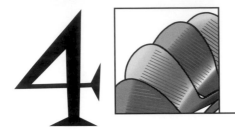

Tommy Armour

Tommy Armour was known as the 'Silver Scot.' A tough competitor, he enjoyed a hugely successful career including victories in the 1927 US Open, 1930 PGA Championship and 1931 Open.

Moving to America in his 30s, he built an unrivalled reputation as a teacher, but was prone to furious outbursts that had even the toughest golfers trembling in fear. A decorated war veteran, he was known to have strangled a German infantryman with his bare hands shortly before losing his sight in one eye during combat.

Not a man to mess with – but one brave soul did. It seemed that Armour, by then a club pro in Chicago, liked to amuse himself taking occasional pot-shots at chipmunks with a .22 calibre rifle he often carried with him during lessons, and it proved a problem when one particular man took offence when he felt his coach was concentrating more on shooting the wildlife than helping him with his slice.

"When are you going to put down that damn gun, Mr Armour, and take care of me?" demanded the irate pupil. Fixing him with his one good eye, the Silver Scot growled: "Don't tempt me, sir, don't tempt me."

5

Tree Trouble
Wilber Artist Stackhouse

Wilber Artist 'Lefty' Stackhouse, **a top tournament pro in the years immediately before** World War Two, had a legendary reputation for on-course eruptions. On one particularly notorious occasion, he was so upset at missing a short putt on the final green of a tournament in Texas that he ran headlong into a tree and knocked himself senseless.

He once leapt into a lake after his ball, but the most famous moment of self-abuse came in 1935, when he was so upset by a hooked drive that he dragged his right hand through a rose bush. Feeling his other hand was mocking him, he dragged that through the bush, too.

Not that age mellowed him any – near the end of his career he was playing in a tournament in Texas when he really lost his temper after a bad shot. Four under par after seven holes, he drove into a lake and the fuse was well and truly lit. Grabbing the bag from his caddie, he calmly walked toward the edge of the water. Launching it into the deep, he followed up by giving his shoes and socks a similarly unusual wash. Then, rolling up his trousers, he stormed off the course, walking straight through a patch of briar nettles.

Missing a Beat
Golfers at the Chandigarh Club
Southern India 1950s

When things go wrong, as they do so often go wrong in golf, caddies are more than used to a little bit of verbal punishment from the golfers they serve. An ear-bashing here or there is all part and parcel of a day's work – but at one Golf Club in Southern India the golfers went a bit too far with their admonishment of caddies, dishing out not so much a tongue lashing, but an actual lashing, if things didn't go as planned.

Not too long ago, golfers at Chandigarh Club were warned against the increasingly common practice of whipping caddies after a bad round. Posted on the club's bulletin board, club manager Sudhar Varma warned members against the extreme actions being carried out, saying, "This is an extremely bad habit, especially on the part of players who are losing. If there are any further reports of caddie-beating, strict disciplinary action will be taken."

7 Fore on the Frontline
British Soldiers. World War One

In 1915, the British Army attempted to end the deadlock of trench war fare in France by forcing a passage through the Dardanelles and forcing Turkey out of the war. A poorly-conceived plan, it ended in failure and humiliation, perhaps best revealed by the attitude of some of the officer corps. Within days of arriving, a rough nine-hole golf course was laid out within sight of the Gallipoli Peninsula.

With the enemy looking on incredulously, young dispatch carriers were drafted in as caddies while the officers played competitions among themselves. Describing the fun, Lieutenant Jenkins wrote: "The best round ever was 42. The going was heavy with much sand, while in other areas there were some very unnatural bunkers of practice trenches and dugouts. The greens were so bad that there was no chance of holing out until the player had manoeuvred his ball within what was called 'a leather of the hole'."

8

Laffoon on the Other Side of His Face
Ky Laffoon

One of the most eccentric golfers in the history of the game is Ky Laffoon, a man who would admonish his clubs for misbehaving after a poor round and even punished them if they carried on annoying him!

On one famous occasion, he offered Ben Hogan a lift from one tournament venue to another in his yellow Cadillac. Falling asleep in the back, Hogan was woken up by a clattering sound coming from the side of the vehicle, and asked Laffoon if there was a problem with the exhaust.

Pulling up by the side of the road, Hogan was astonished to find a putter tied to the door handle by a length of string! "The son-of-a-bitch deserved it!" explained Laffoon calmly as they headed off, with the errant club still rattling down the road for another 300 miles.

The equipment occasionally fought back. Playing in the Sacramento Open in the mid-1930s, he missed a short putt, then slammed the offending club so hard into his foot that the shaft snapped in two... and also broke his toe! Finishing his round, he continued putting out using just the head and a few inches of shaft.

Diagnosed with a terminal illness, he eventually took his own life using a shotgun.

9

Hand Me a Club. Any Club...
Gloria Minoprio
English Ladies Championship at Royal North Devon. October. 1931.

For the short time she played championship golf, Gloria Minoprio had the reputation of being haughty, uncommunicative and arrogant to the point of rudeness as she went from being an unknown talent to become the most talked about golfer of the early 1930's. Then as quickly as she arrived, she disappeared into obscurity, leaving behind few clues as to her real identity or the story behind her rapid rise to fame.

She first came to prominence at the 1931 English Ladies Championship at Royal North Devon, where she scandalised the staid world of British Golf by appearing in a navy blue pullover and matching trousers! Then, after being ushered to the first tee by chauffeur-driven Rolls Royce, she proceeded to play the entire match using just a driving iron.

(With another carried by her liveried caddie In case that one broke!) Considering the difficulty of the high-faced bunkers, it came as no surprise that she lost, but undeterred, she entered the same event three years later at Seacroft in Skegness and won her opening match ...having first practised for two hours each day out of a bunker specially built in the garden of her wealthy lovers' Oxfordshire mansion!

Despite the huge controversy surrounding her bizarre first appearance, Miss Minoprio still chose to wear trousers and use a single club. Aged 27, she also wore heavy white facial makeup, which no doubt inspired Henry Longhurst to describe her "as destitute of emotion as a Frigidaire." Her defeated opponent Betty Sommerville was also not best pleased: "It was like playing a supernatural being," she said afterwards. "She was not a bit friendly... She never spoke once..."

A concert-standard pianist and talented magician, her last competitive appearance came at Royal Portrush in 1939. In typical style, she refused to give any press interviews, and up until her death from septicaemia in 1958, never played golf again.

10

From State Penn to Golf Pin

Henry Brown

October 1876

As requests go it was a rather unusual one. Henry Brown was a talented golfer who wrote to the United States Golf Association asking for a place in the upcoming US Open back in the 1850s. The only problem was that he was serving a jail sentence at the time.

In a persuasive letter, the alimony defaulter outlined a scenario where he would be released for the day from Augusta Penitentiary to play a private 36-hole qualifier in front of nominated officials including the governor of the prison. His caddy would be a guard, and he even agreed to be handcuffed in between shots! Not surprisingly his request was refused. On being released, he filed another entry, and missed qualifying by just a single shot.

CHAPTER TWO

The worst golf chokers

The worst golf chokers

When American Doug Sanders missed that putt on the final green to win the 1970 Open at St Andrews, BBC commentator Henry Longhurst uttered those immortal words: "There but for the grace of God…"

He could not have put it better if he'd tried. There before millions of television viewers, a top golfer had missed a short putt that even the most inexperienced hacker would have fancied his chances of holing.

We all knew what had happened. We all knew how he felt to some degree. Nerves had got the better of him, and he literally choked on the downward stroke, resulting in an ugly stab – and notoriety forever. Up to that point in his career, the colourfully-attired player was being compared in glowing terms to the man he would eventually lose to in the play-off, Jack Nicklaus. That he missed his chance at major-winning immortality is now recorded in the history books, but it does not satisfactorily explain why one hugely-talented golfer will implode under pressure, while another carries on serenely, en route to picking up some of the game's most glittering prizes along the way.

Perhaps the answer can be found in some of the heartbreaking stories in this chapter ….

1

Red-faced at Troon
Bobby Clampett
1982 Open, Royal Troon

Bobby Clampett turned pro in the summer of 1980 to a huge fanfare from the media. Talented, precocious and a supreme putter, here was a kid who could hit shots 200 yards left-handed off his knees.

Two years later, all that promise seemed about to be fulfilled as he took a five-stroke lead at the halfway point of the 1982 British Open at Royal Troon. Dressed in brightly-coloured plus-four trousers, he seemed immune to the pressure of his situation as he extended his lead to seven strokes after five holes of the third round.

Then the wheels began to come off at the longest hole on the Open rota, the par-5, 577-yard sixth hole, where he drove into a fairway bunker. Trying to advance the ball down the fairway, his ball caught the lip and ended up in another bunker. Scrambling his way to the green, he finally carded a triple-bogey eight, and deflated, he limped to the finish line.

After scoring a record 67–66 in the first two rounds, he collapsed to rounds of 78–77, and finished tied tenth. A chastening experience for the young player, it was one his career never really recovered from.

2

Rough Justice
TC Chen
1985 US Open. Oakland Hills

When asked to think of spectacular collapses the mind often goes back to the 1985 US Open at Oakland Hills, Detroit, and an unknown Taiwanese player named 'TC' Chen.

Making his major championship debut, Tze-Chung, as he was known in his home country, had led from the second hole on Thursday – after an albatross two – right up to the fourth hole of the final round on Sunday. The pressure must have been enormous for the five-foot-ten-inch, 140-pound, slow-swinging pro as he was surrounded by television cameras, reporters and photographers all expecting to witness the first Asian winner of a major.

Unfortunately, what they ended up watching was golfing train wreck! Playing the par-4, dogleg fifth, a solid drive was followed by a pushed four-iron into a patch of heavy rough to the right of the green. Attempting to play a splash shot, all he managed to do was go straight under it without moving the ball. Trying again, he double-hit the ball, resulting in a penalty, and he still wasn't on the green. Three shots later he recorded an eight, and practically sleepwalked through the next few holes, dropping shots like confetti. Forever nicknamed 'TC two chip' he never made a serious challenge for a major again.

3

Water Trouble
Jean van de Velde
1999 Open. Carnoustie

Jean van de Velde will long be remembered for his paddling trip on the final hole at Carnoustie during the Open in 1999. Holding a three-shot lead over his nearest rivals, he could take a double-bogey on the hole and still win the Open!

With little guidance from his inexperienced caddie, he threw caution to the wind after his tee-shot found the right-hand rough. Instead of playing safely short of the stream – or burn, as it is known north of the border – that fronted the green, he pulled out a long iron from the bag in an attempt to clear everything. It was a huge mistake – as millions watching on television will testify. After clattering into the grandstand by the green, it rebounded back into even deeper rough, followed by a duff pitch into the water.

Quite what he was thinking next is a complete mystery, as he dragged off his shoes and socks and waded into the fast-flowing water. Hands on hips and ankle-deep in the wet stuff, the bemused-looking Frenchman stood looking at the submerged ball considering his options. Deciding that he had made a big enough fool of himself already, he took a penalty drop followed by another a to a greenside bunker.

Indeed the only thing that stopped this entire episode being played out on golfdisaster.com forever was his up-and-down from the sand that got him into a three-man play-off with Justin Leonard and the eventual winner, Paul Lawrie of Scotland. Taking a triple-bogey seven, when a double bogey would have won you the Open, must be hard to live with, and so it proved for the charismatic Ryder Cup golfer. Suffering from a series of niggling injuries in the years that followed, he never quite managed to recapture the same form, and some time later was invited by a golf magazine to play the same hole using just a putter. He made a six!

4

Aussie Open Freefall
Ian Baker-Finch
1991-1997

Aussie pro Ian Baker-Finch blew away the field to win the British Open at Royal Birkdale in 1991, but within a few years it had all gone horribly wrong. Injuries to his knee, shoulder, and eyes didn't help, and he barely made a halfway cut, missing 11 straight at one point.

Adding insult to injury, every time he finished his round there was always a group of reporters waiting for the latest disaster story. "I dreaded it," he said. "They were always asking negative questions like 'Are you coming out of your slump yet?' My whole life became negative."

He hit rock bottom with a 92 in the opening round of the 1997 Open. He withdrew from the tournament the following day, and quit competitive golf completely by the end of the year. "I lost my confidence," he admitted later. "I got to the point where I didn't even want to be out there because I was playing so poorly."

He now works for American TV, and still plays superbly – though not in tournaments. According to his fellow Aussie pro, Robert Allenby, IBF "could regularly finish in the top 50 on the PGA money list if he could just bring that game inside the ropes."

5

Masters Misery
Greg Norman
US Masters 1996, Augusta National

It was obvious to everyone standing around the final green at the 1996 Masters at Augusta National that Greg Norman was completely shell-shocked. Along with the millions watching on television, they had watched him fritter away a six-stroke lead to his playing partner, Nick Faldo, as he found yet another way of losing the Masters.

It had all been such good news up to that point. The Great White Shark was playing the golf of his life, and seemed an absolute certainty to add a green jacket to his wardrobe. He was even approached by a fellow player in the locker room who said, "Good luck Greg, even you cannot f**k it up from here."

How wrong can you be? Trying to become the first Australian to win the Masters, he hit two balls in the water on the back nine, and lost by five to his greatest rival. Limping home with a round of 78 to Faldo's 67, it produced an 11-shot turnaround and practically rewrote the record books.

"I feel for him," said Faldo. "I hope I'll be remembered for shooting a 67 on the last day and storming through. But obviously, it'll be remembered for what happened to Greg."

6

Guldahl Goes South
Ralph Guldahl and the book that ruined his career

You may have heard of Byron Nelson and Ben Hogan, but what about Ralph Guldahl? One of the greatest golfers of his generation, his fall from glory is still a mystery today.

Born the same year as Hogan, Nelson and Sam Snead, the Texas-born professional dominated golf between 1937 and 1939, winning two U.S. Opens and one Masters. Racking up 16 tournament victories and 19 second-place finishes in a seven-year period dating back to 1933, nobody came close to knocking him off his pedestal as the best golfer on the planet in the years prior to the Second World War.

Then it happened. After his Masters victory at Augusta National in 1939, his golf game literally fell apart, and he never won again. One theory concerns an instructional book that he wrote around this period. A completely natural golfer,

the belief is that he overanalysed his swing, and before you could say "paralysis by analysis", his career was over.

Quitting the Tour in 1942, he returned briefly in 1949, but never recaptured the form that made him such a great player. Three years later he left competitive golf for good, preferring to sell cars in Dallas.

7

Downer for Duval
David Duval loses weight. the girl
- and his game

When David Duval finished the 2002 season down in 80th position on the PGA Tour money list, it proved to be more than just a temporary blip. Once a world Number One, he rarely finished outside the top ten in his first seven years – and he'd won The Open a year earlier. Now, though, he averaged 79 shots per round in the majors, and missed 16 of 20 cuts.

He withdrew from the 2003 PGA Championship at Oak Hill after dropping 16 strokes to par in 22 holes.

At the Hartford Open, he hit four shots out of bounds, including two off the first tee, for an 83.

The reasons behind his massive dip in form remained a mystery, with every golfing pundit from St Andrews to Shinnecock Hills offering their opinion. Even now the real answer is elusive, but the alarm bells began ringing after he split up with his partner of eight years, Julie McArthur, at the beginning of 2002. The substantial weight-loss programme he underwent over the previous two years may have contributed, and things just went from bad to worse.

He quit tournaments for a year, but has yet to recapture the form that made him one of the top golfers in the world.

8

Miller Magic
Whatever happened to Johnny Miller?

Johnny Miller was a golfing phenomenon in the mid-1970s. Competing against the likes of Jack Nicklaus and Tom Watson, this flaxen-haired, rake-thin Californian regularly achieved scores in the low sixties where most thought such figures impossible.

Winner of the 1973 U.S. Open at Oakmont, and 16 other PGA Tour events by the age of 29, Miller confirmed his superstar status by capturing the Open at Royal Birkdale in 1976. However, his career then went into a baffling two-year down-ward spiral, culminating in a 111th-place finish in the 1978 Money List. And while he would come back to win seven more times, the dominance that he had shown a few years earlier was long gone.

Admitting that he "got cocky and stopped practising, stayed at home with my kids", Miller simply lost the will to compete, along with the body shape that had brought him so much success after bulking up in an effort to hit it further.

"When I won the British, I'd won the U.S. Open and shot really low rounds, and had been considered the best player," said Miller, who is currently recognised as the top television golfing pundit in the United States. "Basically I thought I'd done everything I wanted."

9

Troon Trouble
Jesper Parnevik
1997 Open, Royal Troon

Jesper Parnevik held a four-stroke lead during the final round of the 1997 Open at Royal Troon. The only question now was how many shots the eccentric Swede would win by, especially as he had been able to negotiate the testing back nine in five under par for the first three days.

Chased to the wire by the highly-rated American Justin Leonard, Parnevik should have had the result nailed down long before the last few holes, but his reputation for blowing winning leads was not totally undeserved.

At Turnberry in 1994 for example, a double bogey on the 72nd hole enabled Zimbabwean Nick Price to slip in under the wire and win his first Open title. And history repeated itself.

A missed five-footer at 13, a missed three-footer at 16, coupled with some poor approach shots, resulted in five bogeys over the last 13 holes. With victory well and truly out of reach for the oddly-garbed Scandinavian, 25-year old Leonard took full advantage to win by three clear shots.

"This one hurts a little bit more than Turnberry," he said afterwards. "I'd been riding positive momentum all week, and today, I think all the pressure was a bit too much."

10

Choke Hill for Strange
Curtis Strange
1995 Ryder Cup, Oak Hill

Few Ryder Cup matches are clearer in the memory than the crucial **Nick Faldo versus Curtis Strange** tussle at Oak Hill in 1995. Even now, the image of Faldo coolly stroking home his four-foot putt on the final green for victory ranks high in the history of the biannual event.

Yet for every winner there is a loser, and Strange often must have wondered how it ended up being him. Picked as a wild card by his old university buddy and American team captain, Lanny Wadkins, Strange instinctively felt he had something to prove.

No longer the player who won back-to-back US Open titles in 1988–89, the inclusion in the USA side of a 40-something golfer ranked outside the top 50 in the world had already brought carping criticism from sections of the American media, but Wadkins backed the experienced competitor. Wrongly, as it turned out.

Enjoying a narrow lead early in the match, Strange had relinquished any advantage by the time they reached the final green. He made bogey, and lost the hole and the match. "It's a frightening thought," he said afterwards, "how I'm going to feel tomorrow when I wake up."

Almost made the cut

ABSENT MINDED

George Burns found himself thinking the unthinkable prior to the final round of the Tournament Players Championship in 1979. Arriving on the first tee, the burly American pro was only three shots behind tournament leader Lanny Wadkins when he simply forgot how to play golf!

No matter how much he tried, he could not get comfortable enough over the ball to make a swing, and with his playing partners waiting patiently on the tee, the situation was becoming desperate. Eventually he managed to move the ball forward and somehow scrambled around in 83.

Describing it as "the worst day of my life", Burns considered giving up completely, but decided against it. The following week, he scored 67 in the opening round at the Heritage Classic, and the crisis was over.

OLD COURSE HEARTACHE

The notorious Road Hole Bunker, which guards the front of the legendary seventeenth green at St Andrews, has claimed many a victim over the years – including David Duval, who saw his chances of winning the 2000 British Open disappear completely after taking four strokes to escape.

But it is poor Tommy Nakajima from Japan who most people remember. Competing in the 1978 Open, he was attempting to become the first Asian winner of golf's oldest major when he found a sandy grave with his approach in the final round. Also taking four strokes to escape, his name was etched forever in St Andrew's folklore after the bunker was re-christened by one imaginative journalist as "The Sands of Nakajima" – and the name has stuck ever since.

CHAPTER THREE

The worst confrontations and tantrums

47

The worst confrontations and tantrums

Golf is not a game you associate with the on-pitch excesses of football or rugby. Despite being a hugely stressful sport to play at any level, you will travel a long way before you see one golfer square up to another over a missed putt, or a misplaced comment over the quality of his driving.

Of course, you might elicit a brusque comment should you clamber all over an opponent's line with your newly re-spiked Footjoys, but rarely does it escalate into anything more than that. On a really bad day, the average golfer may turn the air blue after running up a card-wrecking dirty dozen on the final hole of the club medal, but even that is usually forgivable.

That is why the following tales from the wonderful world of golf are so shocking. From Arnold Palmer's unseemly Ryder Cup spat with the legendary Ben Hogan, to Old Tom Morris risking a full-blown riot because of his stubborn refusal to play on, can we ever look at the Royal and Ancient Game in quite the same way again?

1

Florida Fracas
Club golfers
1998. Breakers Golf Club. Florida

Four golfers set off for an early-morning round at the Breakers Golf Club in Palm Beach County, Florida in June 1998. With no-one in front, tempers became frayed as one of them complained about the slow pace of play. Storming off ahead, his erstwhile partners shrugged their shoulders, expecting to meet up with him at the 19th.

Two hours later, there was no sign of him. Finding his car in the parking lot, a club official was informed and the search was on. Adding to the mystery, his clubs were then found abandoned near the seventh green.

Three days later, an aged crocodile named 'Ol' Mose' was spotted on the same hole, and became an immediate suspect. After much discussion between the local police force, state lawyers and even the American Crocodile Association, it was decided to open up the old reptile and take a peek. Fortunately there was no sign of the errant golfer. He eventually turned up a few days later wearing a very sheepish look.

2

Ryder Cup Row
Arnold Palmer and Ben Hogan
1967 Ryder Cup. Champions Club. Texas

Few golfers ever got the better of Arnold Palmer head-to-head in the Ryder Cup. His outstanding record of just two defeats in 32 matches is testimony to his skill and nerve. Yet while almost everyone adored the dashing 'Arnie', his 1967 Ryder Cup team captain, Ben Hogan, certainly did not.

Prior to the match, Hogan decided that his team would play with the smaller British-size golf ball because it better suited the windy conditions. Having flown non-stop from his home at Latrobe, Pennsylvania, Arnie never got the news, and turned up on the practice ground totally unprepared for the change. Asking Hogan for a box of balls to practise with, his captain growled back ungraciously, "What for? You haven't made the team yet."

Two days later, the great man was inexplicably 'rested' from the morning four-ball matches, despite having won both his foursomes matches with Gardner Dickinson the day before.

The press demanded to know why, but Hogan's lips were sealed.

It later transpired that Palmer had given a lift in his private jet to British professional Tony Jacklin, which according to Hogan was totally unforgivable and tantamount to fraternising with the 'enemy'. Not surprisingly, the two golfing legends enjoyed a frosty relationship for some time to come.

The Ryder Cup at Kiawah Island in 1991 will long be remembered as the 'War On The Shore' for its unprecedented intensity. Played on the newly-constructed Ocean Course in South Carolina, an outraged Seve Ballesteros accused Paul Azinger of cheating on the opening day, and temperatures remained at boiling point throughout the week – and beyond.

Ultimately, the entire match swung on a missed five-foot putt by Bernhard Langer on the final green of the final match, giving the USA a narrow one-point victory. One local sportswriter summed up the feeling of many Americans and a hugely partisan crowd when he wrote, "We're hot. We're on a roll. Check it out. We thumped Iraq. We whipped Communism. And now, at last, we put Europe in its place."

4

Don't you Know Who I am?
Jack Nicholson
1994

The Golf course has long offered celebrities a little 'down' time away from the public spotlight.

Offering a few precious hours away from autograph-hunting fans and paparazzi cameramen, stars like Clint Eastwood, Bill Murray and Sean Connery are known to flock to the links every time there is a break in filming. Even when they are working, Michael Douglas and his wife Catherine Zeta Jones enjoy rubbing shoulders with golfers like Ernie Els and Tiger Woods by competing in the annual Bob Hope Classic Pro-am tournament held for many years at Pebble Beach. Another name who enjoys the annual 'clambake' event is the legendary Jack Nicholson, who has played in the tournament many times over the years. Unfortunately, the star of 'A Few Good Men' attracted headlines of another sort when he found himself before a Los Angeles judge after a traffic incident in early 1994. Pleading guilty at the resultant court case, he was alleged to have grabbed a five-iron out of his trunk before threatening a motorist who cut him up in traffic! Feeling a little put out, all the gravel-voiced actor would comment afterwards was, "I should have used the driver on the son-of-a-bitch."

5

Fürer's Fury
Adolf Hitler
1936 Olympic Games

Adolf Hitler had good reason to dislike golf. Having poured a small fortune into developing the game in Germany in the five years prior to the outbreak of World War Two, including providing low-cost equipment and free lessons for the masses, he was scheduled to present the trophy for a post-Olympic Games golf tournament in 1936.

Heading for the spa town of Baden-Baden, the German pair were well ahead with one round to play. Victory would perhaps placate the Chancellor, who was still smarting from the gold medals Jesse Owens – who definitely didn't fit the Aryan stereotype – won a few days earlier.

Unfortunately for the Führer, the English partnership of Arnold Bentley and Antony Thirsk hadn't read the Nazi script, and came from nowhere to win the large brass salver inlaid with semi-precious stones. Somebody had to tell him, and the unenviable task fell to his Government Minister, Von Ribbentrop.

Enraged, Hitler flounced back to his car, telling Von Ribbentrop that if anyone was going to present the English pair with their prize it would have to be him! The ceremony went ahead, but the tournament was never held again. The trophy resided for the next fifty years at Hesketh Golf Club, the home of Bentley and Thirsk.

6

Who do you Think you are Kidding Mr Hitler?
Douglas Grant
3rd September 1939, Royal St George's Golf Club

Britain declared war on Germany at 11.00 a.m. on September 3rd, 1939. An hour earlier, a members' four-ball, including former captain Douglas Grant, had teed off from the first at Royal St George's in Sandwich.

The dire news was due to come through on the wireless, and Grant demanded that the club steward run the flag up the pole should war be declared during the round. By the time they reached the tenth tee, the Red Cross of St George was flying proudly next to the clubhouse, but they decided to continue with their game.

A few minutes later, Grant was at the top of his swing when an air-raid siren went off, causing him to shank his ball into a bunker. Red-faced with anger, he ordered his caddie to pick up the ball. "If this damn war is going to spoil my golf," he roared, "I will pop over to Germany and have a word with Herr Hitler myself!"

Not that war fazed golfers at one south-coast course in 1940. With the threat of German paratroopers landing any moment, they issued a local rule that it was now legal to flaunt the 14-club maximum allowance by adding a rifle or shotgun to the bag!

What a Burke

Arnold Palmer and Jackie Burke

1967 Ryder Cup

In the 1967 Ryder Cup at the Champions Club in Texas, Arnold Palmer was paired with Julius Boros in the second-day afternoon four-balls against arguably the weakest players in the British side, George Will and Hugh Boyle. It was a game the Americans were expected to win easily, but the British pair stunned the hosts.

Scoring well, they were four holes up at the turn, and looked set for a spectacular victory. Walking towards the 10th tee, a dejected Arnie was greeted by American vice-captain Jackie Burke, who taunted his lack of success in the match, saying, "Well, Palmer. I've heard about these famous charges of yours. Let me see you get out of this one. In fact, if you win, I'll hand-build you a clock to stick in your house."

Palmer took this as a personal challenge. Hitching up his trousers in typical Arnie fashion, he made par at the tenth to win the hole. A three-iron approach within tap-in range at the 466-yard, 11th cut the British lead down to 2-up. Another birdie followed at the par-five 13th, and a third in four holes at the next. The final result – Palmer and Boros won by 1-up. Arnie got his clock – and Burke felt like one.

8

Roaming Ronan
Ronan Rafferty
1991 US Open

Now a respected television pundit, Northern Irish professional Ronan Rafferty was quite a firebrand in his younger years. A former European Number One and Ryder Cup golfer, he was granted a special exemption to play in the 1991 United States Open.

Struggling with his game, Ronan was 11 strokes over par halfway through his second round when he just had enough. Partnered with Craig Parry and Corey Pavin, he informed referee Ed Gowan that he was quitting, but the message never got through to his playing partners, who thought he was attending a call of nature in some nearby trees.

By the time they had finished their round, Rafferty was already at the airport ready to board his flight home! Unfortunately for the maverick golfer, he faced further trouble on his return – he was severely reprimanded by the European Tour for his unsportsmanlike behaviour.

9

Thunder and Lightning
Eric Brown and Tommy Bolt
1957 Ryder Cup

Scottish professional Eric Brown was a workmanlike golfer, but competitive to his fingertips. In the 1957 Ryder Cup in Yorkshire, he found himself matched in the singles against the equally fiery American, Tommy 'Lightning' Bolt.

Adding spice to the occasion, Brown had read in a newspaper article that "the British team has absolutely no hope of beating the USA", despite trailing by just two points going into the final day. With the story tucked in his golf bag, he set about proving the sneerers wrong.

Accompanied by the largest crowd of the day, Bolt quickly began to complain about their partisan behaviour. "They cheered when I missed a putt," he said bitterly, "and sat on their hands when I hit a good shot".

With Britain well ahead, and with holes starting to run out for the Americans, Bolt's patience finally snapped, along with the shaft of his five-iron, which he bent over his knee in frustration.

Winning by 4&3, Brown offered his hand in consolation to his opponent as it became obvious that Great Britain had won the Ryder Cup. Turning away in disgust, Bolt said how little he had enjoyed the game. "Neither would I mate, if I'd just received the hammering you just had!" a gleeful Brown replied.

10

Bombing it down the Middle
James Sheridan and some German Bombers
1940. Sunningdale

James Sheridan, legendary caddie master at Sunningdale, decided to help out the green keeper by mowing the 18th green on the Old Course in 1940. He had covered just over half of it when he heard the drone of German aircraft nearby.

Suddenly, a huge explosion came from over the road on the ladies' course. Another bomb exploded just 200 yards away down the fairway, and Mr Sheridan realised the devices were landing in a line. Diving for cover, he threw himself into the bunker on the right-hand side of the green.

As he did so, another bomb fell short of the green to the left. In the next three minutes, some 100 bombs rained down on the golf course and surrounding area. It seemed some German bombers had been attacked by Spitfires, and had immediately ditched their bombs for a speedy escape. With the clubhouse barely touched, the indomitable Sheridan climbed out of his greenside bunker, dusted himself down, and finished mowing the green.

CHAPTER FOUR

The worst controversies

61

The worst controversies

Scandals and controversy are concepts alien to golf – usually. Unlike other sports like boxing, you cannot imagine players taking a metaphorical dive to lose an important match, any more than you can picture top golfers selling a kiss-and-tell-story, as in the soccer world. Yet the Royal and Ancient game has seen its fair share of controversial moments over the years, as this chapter reveals.

With the advent of Tiger Woods, golf is now big news, and for the scandal-hungry media, the off-course antics of some professionals have provided some very juicy headlines. Part of the price of fame is the movement from back page to front page. Of course, it was not always the case.

Up until the advent of televised golf in the early 1960s, golf was considered 'whiter than white' in sporting terms. Twenty years on, there was still an honourable truce between golf and the media, and while controversial moments were reported, many others, especially those concerning the private lives of players, were quietly shelved because publication was not deemed to be in the best interests of the game.

Today it is a free-for-all. Controversy sells newspapers, and scandal is the lifeblood of many a hack journalist. Golf is no longer the elite sport it once was. Its ever-increasing popularity has led to journalists searching out ever more novel and testosterone-fuelled ways to report on the game. So goodness only knows what they would have done with some of the stories that follow from the game's past…

1

Leaping Lehman
Ryder Cup.
Brookline 1999.

The press named it the 'Battle of Brookline', as the Ryder Cup at Brookline Country Club in 1999 turned out to be one of the most controversial matches in the event's 72-year history. A tense affair all week, things really kicked off after members of the USA team stampeded onto the seventeenth green after Justin Leonard holed a monster putt that would ultimately win the prize for the home team.

With his opponent Jose Maria Olazabal still waiting to putt, Sam Torrance viewed the scene with utter horror – especially the part Tom Lehman played in it. Watching the former British Open Champion and committed Christian whooping with delight, he turned to an on-course commentator and said, "and he calls himself a man of God". Interestingly, Lehman was later appointed Ryder Cup captain for 2006.

2 Rumours of my Death Have Been Greatly Exaggerated

A newspaper report in 1917 shocked the golfing world when it described how five-time Open champion James Braid had met with a fatal accident at Waterloo Station in London.

Along with Harry Vardon and John Henry Taylor, he had dominated golf around the turn of the century, and was instrumental in establishing the Professional Golfers' Association before being employed as Club Professional at the prestigious Walton Heath Golf Club in Surrey.

As clubhouses all over Britain lowered their flags out of respect for the fallen champ, the story was rapidly withdrawn as it was found to be untrue. In a strange mixture of coincidences, a James A. Braid of Southsea had been killed while running for a train in London, and another former Open Champion, Bob Martin, had died of old age at his home near St. Andrews. By the time it took to correct the report, a memorial service for the still healthy Braid had already been booked for Winchester Cathedral.

3 Bye Bye Birdie

Imagine a world with no golf: a world where just stepping out on the links was a criminal offence. Well, that was the situation back in 1457, after King James II outlawed the sport in Scotland because its growing popularity was interfering with the citizens' archery practice!

With the English army threatening to invade from the south, fines were imposed for anyone over 12 who did not attend at least three times a week. Repeating the ban in 1491, his descendant James IV was petitioned by golf-mad nobles to nullify the decree, but the monarch would not budge, describing it as 'a ridiculous sport requiring neither strength or skill, and properly should be abandoned".

4 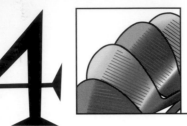 Moody Monty

Colin Montgomerie has found that praise for his golfing brilliance is often followed by carping criticism for his on-course demeanour. He's too sullen, they said. Why didn't he smile more? Yet over the years, Monty had learned to take such matters in his stride.

A perfectionist at heart, his uncompromising attitude to failure remains both his best and possibly most misunderstood asset. In 1997 for example, he began the season with a $1million victory in the Anderson Consulting Match Play tournament, and ended with a record fifth European Order of Merit title.

Yet the season also had its downside and not a little controversy. In the US Masters in April, the Scottish pro har-rumphed his way out of the tournament after closing with a nightmare round of 81. Blown away by the big-hitting Tiger Woods in the third round, the Augusta Chronicle described him as "a rumpled Scotsman who is a killer in Europe but can't get arrested in the United States". Still, anything was better than being called "Mrs Doubtfire" for the millionth time.

5

Charging the Crowd
Ryder Cup 1933

Few sporting events can match the Ryder Cup for sheer drama, excitement and controversy. Played since 1927, it is golf at its dramatic best with victory or defeat often depending on the outcome of a single game. That, at least, was the case at Southport and Ainsdale Golf Club in 1933. Playing in front of record crowds, the Britain and Ireland team needed only a share of the final-day singles to pull off an unexpected victory. Watched by the heir to the British throne, Edward, Prince of Wales, the entire match balanced on a knife-edge all afternoon until it came down to the final game between Englishman Syd Easterbrook and American Densmore Shute.

The atmosphere was electric as the crowd, whipped into a nationalistic frenzy by the appearance of the future King, began to encroach onto the fairways causing some of the American players to complain. Without any ropes to hold them back, a bad situation got worse when the stewards started charging at the gallery, stabbing at them with pointed sticks with red and white flags at the end.

Employed to signal where the ball landed, they earned themselves the nickname of 'the Southport Lancers'. In scenes reminiscent of modern-day Ryder Cup matches, Shute missed from three feet on the last, leaving his opponent a simple tap-in for an overall victory by 6½ – 5½. At the presentation ceremony, the Prince summed up the feelings of everyone there when he said, "In giving this Cup, I am naturally impartial, but of course, we over here are very pleased to have won".

6 Hamming it up

Golf is known for its sportsmanlike behaviour between opponents, but sometimes you can take it too far. Playing in an international match between Scotland and England in 1948, top Scottish amateur Hamilton McInally was four up after nine holes against his out-of-sorts opponent.

Deciding to give him a quick lesson, it obviously had the desired effect, because his playing partner played a lot better, and the match looked like it might go down to the eighteenth. Questioned by his increasingly red-faced team captain on the seventeenth green about why it had gone so far, 'Hammy' replied, "I showed him what he was doing wrong and now we are having a real fine game!" His reply is not recorded but we can hazard a guess it was not too complimentary.

7

Groovy baby
The Open.
Royal Troon. 1923.

The 1923 Open at Royal Troon became a battleground between defending champion Walter Hagen and the tournament organisers. Trouble began less than 36 hours before the opening round, when the R&A outlawed any iron-headed club that had small round dots cut into the club's face to aid backspin.

As this was common practice in the USA, Hagen decided to speak out in the press describing it as "completely unsportsmanlike" But the championship committee would not budge over the ban and like his fellow countrymen, he spent most of the night before the opening round filing the faces of his iron-clubs smooth!

Finishing runner-up to Englishman Arthur Havers, the outspoken American refused to take part in the trophy presentation ceremony because his fellow professionals had been banned from the clubhouse all week. Hagen told reporters, "I am sorry to say that I did not receive the sort of treatment which would make me anxious to return". Despite his comments, Hagen did return the following year to win his second Open title at Royal Liverpool.

8

Ladies First
Walton Heath & Sunningdale. 1910.

An unusual 'battle-of-the-sexes' challenge match was arranged over Walton Heath and Sunningdale in 1910 between top woman golfer, Cecilia Leitch, and the top male golfer of the age, Harold Hilton.

Watched by thousands of onlookers, it was arranged that both players would drive from the men's tees, but Leitch was compensated for her lack of strength by receiving a handicap allowance of one stroke, every second hole. After four rounds in front of a large, mainly female gallery, Leitch won by the narrow margin of 2 and 1.

Not surprisingly, the match received a great deal of publicity, played as it was during a time when women's rights were at the forefront of the political agenda, and the Suffragette movement was at its height. A hugely controversial result, it was hailed as a triumph for women, and the Suffragettes lost little time in publicising the victory. Not surprisingly, the red-faced Hilton adamantly refused any talk of a rematch.

9

Royal Rumpus

Away from the closeted world of royal life, Edward, Prince of Wales (later King Edward VIII) enjoyed the company of golfers. A reputedly shy man, he played and socialised with many of the top golfers of the day, including Bobby Jones and Walter Hagen.

Never one to stand on ceremony, the story is told that, after a game at a fashionable club in Surrey, he invited English professional Archie Compston into the clubhouse for a drink. Apologising profusely, the club secretary then informed the Royal visitor that professionals were not allowed inside, and he would have to remain on the verandah.

Spinning on his heels. Edward marched out of the door saying, "if it is not good enough for my guest, it is not good enough for me". Unlike many other Golf Clubs he patronised, the one in question never did receive its 'royal' title.

10 One for the Road

Challenge matches between professionals became increasingly popular in the second half of the 19th century, with huge sums riding on the outcome of individual or matched pairs. Like the bare-knuckle fights of the same period, they were well-supported, with the most popular matches being those between Tom Morris of St Andrews and his great rival, Willie Park of Musselburgh.

With vast sums bet on the outcome, the large galleries were not averse to a little skulduggery to influence the result. At Musselburgh in 1855 for example, a match between Morris and Park threatened to turn into a riot after supporters began kicking 'Old' Tom's ball into the rough.

He refused to play on, and retired to a nearby pub, Mrs Foreman's, while the police tried to achieve some order. Park then told Morris that unless he continued with the match he would claim the £500 prize money! Morris declined, and Park played on alone, with those who had bet on the St Andrews man crying foul. Grabbing the money as he holed out on the final green, he was extremely fortunate to escape with his life.

Almost made the cut

TROPHY TIPPLE

Scottish-born professional Fred Herd won the United States Open Championship at Myopia in 1898. Remarkably, such was his hard-drinking reputation that the organisers required him to put up some security before they would release the silver trophy to him. It was feared he might pawn it!

THE BOTTOM LINE

During the Ryder Cup at Muirfield in 1973, a supremely confident Lee Trevino boasted he would "kiss the American team's asses" unless he beat European number one, Peter Oosterhuis in their singles match the following day. The record book shows that he halved the match and his team members – including Jack Nicklaus and Arnold Palmer – insisted that he kept his promise.

Almost made the cut

LOCKED-OUT LEGEND

Challenging for the lead in the British Open at Royal Lytham in 1926, Bobby Jones arrived at the course for the final round minus his player's badge. Despite being the most recognisable golfer on the planet, he was refused entry by a gateman, and had to pay out one shilling to gain admission! Taking this minor setback in his stride, the American eventually went on to win the tournament.

GREEN FOR DANGER

Hubert Green, whose swing was once described as "an octopus trying to hit a ball inside a telephone booth", was leading the US Open at Southern Hills in 1977. Staying at a nearby hotel, he received a knock on the door from the local police chief, who told him about a death threat they had received. Holding a one-stroke lead, he steadfastly refused to pull out, and appeared untroubled by the small army of state troopers and police sharpshooters who followed his every move as he held on to win his first major championship.

CHAPTER FIVE

The world's worst courses

The world's worst courses

So what makes for a pleasant round of golf? Many would agree with the 1950s amateur champion, Robert Harris, who wrote: 'The hazards and bumps on the course are there to offer a challenge to the skill, courage and philosophy of the player, who suffers no interference in his game except from nature.'

But golf has changed immeasurably over the past half-century. When he talks about suffering 'no interference in his game except from nature', do you think he envisaged golf courses with live crocodiles as part of the landscape? Or movable floating greens?

Traditional courses, with their sweeping fairways and gently-contoured greens, are no longer enough for some modern-day golfers. Many are looking for a new challenge to occupy their time – a more extreme form of the game, where the rough is home to deadly reptiles and the bunkers have quicksand in them! Traversing the world in search of courses to play, they seek out the searing-hot deserts of Death Valley one day, and the icy wastes of Greenland the next.

Perhaps Sam Snead got it right when he said: "Golf-course architects make me sick. They can't play themselves, so they rig the courses so nobody else can play either."

With that in mind, he would have loved this chapter…

1

Animal Crackers
North Star Golf Club
Alaska

If you want to combine golf with a touch of animal spotting, then North Star Golf Club in Fairbanks, Alaska is probably the place to go. Built in 1991, it is just 200 miles from the Arctic Circle, and resembles a Scottish links... when it is not covered in 12 inches of snow!

It's open just four months a year, and the wind chill factor makes playing a round here almost unbearable. Even with those five layers of woollen jumpers to protect you from the cold, howling forty-mile-an-hour winds, combined with an average temperature of minus 26°C in December, definitely make this a place to avoid in the winter months.

Even in summer, this is definitely not Augusta National. Built on permafrost, it resembles a green moonscape in parts, with humps, hollows and the occasional irritable moose wandering. You can also spot grizzly bears, wolves and eagles.

It remains the only course in the world where you pick up two score-cards on the first tee – one for keeping a record of your round, and the other a guide to local wildlife. It does have one advantage though – with 24 hours of daylight, booking a tee-time is never a problem!

2

The Peak of Fitness
Socorro Peak
New Mexico

Just the one hole – but, it's two-and-a-half miles, offers unbelievable views and is downhill all the way!

That is what awaits any golfer turning up at the first (and only) tee for the Elfego Baca 'Shoot', a whacky competition held down the side of the Socorro Peak for an insane group of Extreme Golf nuts.

Limited to just ten golfers a time, you'll need comprehensive injury insurance, because this is no easy stroll among the azaleas. Intrepid golfers set off for the peak by jeep at 6am, and rip it all the way down the slope!

Each player is allowed just one ball – but three friends can act as ball-spotters to help find spheres lost among the prickly pear cacti, disused mine shafts, and sharp-as-a-razor rocky outcrops. Scorpions and rattlesnakes also pervade this corner of the world.

Accompanied by a score keeper who is thankfully a trained first aid expert, you smash your opening drive off a tiny wooden platform down the Rio Grande valley, go and find it, then hit it again.

Dropping 2,550 feet in elevation, broken limbs are not unheard of as players slip and slide their way down the slope towards a large white painted circle at the bottom known imaginatively as the 'hole'. The winner is the one who takes fewest shots… and who comes down the mountain in one piece.

3  Pushing the Boat Out
Coeur d'Alene
Idaho

One of the most photographed par 3 holes in the world, the short 14th is a floating island green at Coeur d'Alene made of honeycombed concrete, filled with Styrofoam and topped off with real topsoil and grass. Ranging in distance from 145 yards to 220 yards depending on the breezy winds that can whip across this part of the North West United States, the green is pulled in and out from the shore by thick metal cables.

For those golfers confused about what club to hit, a caddie measures the exact distance with the aid of a laser gun. Unlike the notorious seventeenth hole at the Players Club at Ponte Vedra, Florida, this green is only accessible by a small wooden craft imaginatively named the 'water boat'.

Each golfer is only allowed two tee-shots before he must take a penalty drop on the actual island next to the putting green. A sensible option to help speed up play – but whether golfers keep to this local rule is another thing. Probably not – the course owners drag well over 40,000 balls from the lake each year… from just 30,000 rounds! And somebody must be able to hit the green in regulation!

4

Watch the Birdie
Battle Lake Golf Club
Texas

As a young boy, Tiger Woods was taught to keep his concentration – no matter what distractions he faced. Hitting balls into a net as a ten-year-old, father Earl would shout, scream and bang a drum on his down-swing in the hope of putting him off. But even Tiger might have trouble concentrating at the Battle Lake Golf Club in Mart, Texas, after owner Chuck Higgins came up with a unique way of attracting male golfers to his course.

Hoping to reverse a steady decline in green-fee income, in 2004 he began employing scantily-clad young women dressed in "eye-catching outfits" as beverage cart drivers, pro-shop assistants, first-tee greeters and snack-bar attendants.

Nick-named the 'Birdie Girls', they proved a big hit with visiting green-fee payers. After a six-year decline, revenues shot up in line with the shortness of the skirts. The country and western music that blares out of the clubhouse obviously goes down well, but is it any wonder that the club was labelled 'the hardest course in Texas to keep your eye on the ball'.

5  Sign Here Please
Hans Merensky Country Club
South Africa

The most hazardous thing most British green
keepers have to do is rake the bunkers and
brush away a few errant tree branches, but it's
a very different story at the Hans Merensky Country
Club in South Africa.

There, some brave soul has to clear the course
of everything from water buffalo to warthogs,
crocodiles to cheetahs and hippos to hyenas. Not
to mention three types of deadly snake usually
infesting the rough – including the Mozambique
spitting cobra that can launch a venomous attack

from over ten feet away.

Nobody is allowed on the 18-hole course before 7am or after 4.30pm. Even then, each visitor is asked to sign an indemnity clause before they play, releasing the club from any responsibility just in case anyone gets stung, bitten, attacked, maimed, savaged or possibly eaten. And just in case you thought you were safe behind the electric fence that borders the two properties, the authorities have included a number of small holes – called 'cradles' – to allow smaller animals like baboons, deer and the occasional lioness unimpeded access to the water on the course.

Remarkably, they have thousands of green fee visitors a year, but only one recorded fatality, and that was the result of a charging elephant protecting her young!

6 Santa Claus Country Club

Uummaanq

Greenland

The annual World Ice Golf Championship held in March at Uummaanq, Greenland, always attracts a good entry despite being played in one of the most inhospitable places on the planet.

Situated 400 miles inside the Arctic Circle, the tournament is played on a glacier with compacted snowdrifts acting as backdrops. Play starts early in the morning, and with the exception of chipping and putting, each shot can be teed up, as long as it falls between the markers that denote the fairways.

With typical temperatures of minus 15° to 25°, you'll require thermal underwear, ski masks and goggles – and of course red golf balls, which often dip in flight as it ices up through the air. The organisers also advise people to leave their graphite-shafted clubs at home because cold makes them brittle and they can shatter on impact.

With greens called 'whites', the layout is short by modern standards at just under 2,780 yards. Not surprisingly, the rules of golf are liberally interpreted. Competitors are allowed to brush loose snow away from the line of their putt, but the tournament committee is still awaiting a ruling from the R&A regarding interference from the polar bears that occasionally visit the area!

7

A Good Walk Spoiled
Mongolia

Mongolia is probably best known for Genghis Khan and his hordes, yaks and an ancient form of polo where an enemy's head substituted for the ball. It is definitely not known for golf!

Back in 2000, an intrepid hacker named André Tolme took a club and a few balls, and decided he would play his way across 1,319 miles of barren country from Choybalsan to Dund-Us in the name of charity – a trip that took months rather than weeks. He first came up with this whacky idea two years earlier, when he visited Mongolia and figured the flat grassy terrain would be perfect for golf.

Financing the trip by letting people sponsor his golf balls at $25 a pop, he estimated that he used up to 420 of them over an estimated distance of 2.3 million yards. Tolme said he'd met people who cycled, walked or jogged across a country, but nobody who'd golfed such a distance.

Perhaps he should have met golf nut Floyd Rood. A few years earlier, he played his way across mainland United States, travelling approximately 3,400 miles. He hit 114,737 shots (including 3,511 penalty shots) and wore out a dozen pairs of golf shoes!

8

Stamping Your Card
Royal Troon. Scotland

The short par-3, eighth hole at Royal Troon in Scotland was described by the golf correspondent for the Glasgow Herald newspaper as 'the worst golf hole I ever saw!'

Visiting in 1910, he berated the committee and golf professional Willie Fernie for moving the green 50 yards forward, leaving a blind tee-shot to a narrow plateau green set into the side of a steep, grassy bank.

Known as the 'Postage Stamp' because of its tiny landing area, it is the shortest and undoubtedly best-known short hole on the Open rota.

What would Fernie have made of the feature added since his visit in 1910 – nearby Prestwick Airport? The runway is behind the tenth tee, making it the noisiest hole in championship golf. At the 2004 Open, some planes flew so low that the giant television cranes used by the BBC were raised and lowered on orders from the Airport Tower.

As an extra safety feature, camera operators were in constant radio contact so they knew exactly when these planes were flying over. With Concorde a regular visitor to this part of Scotland a few years back, visiting golfers were even offered earplugs on the first tee whenever it was expected to fly over.

9

Barbed Wire, Bullets and Birdies
Stalag Luft III
Poland

While golf was played at a number of POW camps in Germany, the best known was Stalag Luft III in modern-day Poland. Home to the legendary 'Great Escape', in which 76 Allied servicemen tunnelled out in March 1944, an eighteen-hole 'course' was constructed with small sandy greens and rusty tomato cans hammered into the hard ground as the cup.

Using an antique wooden-shafted club, holes ranged in distance between 50 and 70 yards. The course even had its own 'brown-keeper', who was given the task of removing stones and smoothing the sand by hand each day. But the camp guards became suspicious about the extra amount of 'contouring' going on.

Persuaded to let play continue, another problem was the camp perimeter fence. With one particular hole situated near a ten-yard strip of land between the inner and outer fences, it was inevitable that many balls would land inside this so-called 'death zone'.

Most definitely out-of-bounds, guards toted machine guns – and used them. But with golf and football played all day during summer, it was inevitable that some balls would fly over the trip-wire into this deadly No Man's Land. To show that those fetching them weren't trying to escape – for now – they wore white butcher's coats.

10

Native Americans
Nine-Hole Nightmare
Oka Golf Club
Canada

Native Americans really went on the warpath in 1990, when the Oka Golf Club in Canada revealed plans to extend their nine-hole course onto land used as a Mohawk Reservation.

Attempting to hold the developers off by force, a barricade was erected on a nearby bridge, severely disrupting commuter traffic in the Montreal area. The local authorities responded by blocking the delivery of food, water and essential fuel supplies, leading to a tense stand-off between the Mohawks and the Canadian army.

With golfers warned to stay well away from Oka Golf Club, the situation took a tragic turn when a local policeman was killed during a gun battle. Thankfully, common sense prevailed, as the disputed land was purchased by the Canadian Government before handing it back to the tribes.

SLAMMIN' SAM RAILROADED OUT OF TOWN
St Andrews, Scotland

Shaped like a shepherd's crook and occupying a narrow finger of land bordered by the Eden estuary and St Andrews Bay, the Old Course remains the most famous 18 holes of golf in the world.

A true sporting Mecca, every legend of the game, from Old Tom Morris to Harry Vardon, Bobby Jones to Arnold Palmer, has walked its fairways, and nowhere in the world does six centuries of golf history come alive like it does in this small corner of Fife.

Yet despite its mythical reputation, not everyone falls instantly under the St Andrews spell, and an honest golfer might tell you that the Old Course can prove a touch disappointing first time out.

One legend who certainly found St Andrews not to his liking was Samuel Jackson Snead, who saw it for the first time in 1946. At that first post-war Open, the links was not looking its best, and it prompted a question about "the abandoned old golf course" he could see from his railway carriage. To which a crusty old Scot replied: "That, sir, is the Royal and Ancient Golf Club of St Andrews, founded in 1754 and is not now, nor ever will be, abandoned".

TANKS FOR THE MEMORY
Kabul Golf Club, Afghanistan

It sounds like a real bargain: a quiet-as-a-grave golf course and only $60 a year to join. That is the bargain on offer at the Kabul Golf Club in Afghanistan. Tempted? Situated in the mountains above the capital, the only problems between you and an idyllic game of golf are loose impediments like unexploded bombs, razor wire and bullet casings littering the fairways. At least that was the case in 2002 before the nine-hole course was liberated by American troops en route to kicking out the fundamentalist Taliban Government.

With burned-out Russian tanks acting as a backdrop, it was closed ten years before by a local warlord, who thought all sport was un-Islamic. Now it has its own professional/greenkeeper, Mohammad Afzal Abdul, and enough Western finance to see it through the next few years. Now, where is that membership form?

ARCTIC ANTICS
Green Zone Golf Club, North Pole

Ever feel you want to get more from your weekly game of golf? Get your clubs, slip on some snowshoes and five layers of clothing, and head up to the Green Zone Golf Club near the North Pole.

There's a problem – you only play it a few weeks a year, you can never get a caddie and the ball-washers keep freezing up! But at least you can tell people that you hit the ball so far, you knocked it out of the country, as it includes one hole where the tee is in Sweden and the green in Finland! Boasting its own customs office, it offers sunlight 24 hours a day from June to August, and is played over two time zones.

CHAPTER SIX

The worst luck

The worst luck

Nick Faldo does not believe it exists, and Walter Hagen swore by it. So how much does luck play in a round of golf? A little? A lot? Or none at all? Speaking as someone who constantly berates the fates for the amount of bad bounces I have during a typical eighteen holes, I have a particular interest in the subject.

If I need the ball to bounce left, it bounces right into sand. If I need a putt to drop, it rims out – and at the end of every round, I can account for at least a dozen strokes that might have been saved had Lady Luck been on my side.

To make matters worse, I have a golfing pal who must own a field full of four-leaf clovers, because his ball runs through bunkers, hops over ditches and never goes out of bounds. On the tree-lined layout we play on as members, the course often resembles an arboreal pinball machine – his ball consistently ends up in the middle of the fairway, no matter how wild his tee-shots!

Thankfully, unlike many of the players featured in this chapter, I no longer play the game for a living. If I did, I'm sure I'd be in no fit mental state to communicate their stories to you...

1

He should have waited until the nineteenth hole

Harry Bradshaw

1949 British Open

Most golfers enjoy a cold bottle of beer in the club-house, but not many have lost a major tournament because of a bottle of beer! Early in the second round of the 1949 Open at Royal St George's, Harry Bradshaw sliced his drive on the fifth and unluckily found his ball inside the bottom half of a discarded brown ale bottle.

Pondering the lie for a short time he decided to smash it out rather than refer to the rulebook – which would have given him a free drop under the outside agency ruling. Able to advance it just a few yards down the fairway, the resultant double bogey cost him outright victory, and he narrowly lost an eighteen-hole play-off to South African Bobby Locke the following day. Sadly, the Irishman never came close to winning again. Possibly a case of shaken but not stirred.

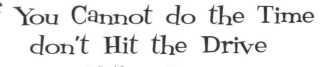

2 If You Cannot do the Time don't Hit the Drive

Mathieu Boya

Benin 1987

Mathieu Boya hit the most expensive shot in history while practising next to the Benin Air Base in 1987. Striking a bird with a particularly fierce drive, the unfortunate creature landed in the open cockpit of a Mirage jet fighter taxiing along the runway. The unexpected visitor frightened the life out of the pilot, causing him to lose control of the jet, smashing into four other jet fighters parked on the ground and practically wiping out the entire Benin Airforce in one blow. The estimated cost of the damage was $200 million. Boya for his trouble was later jailed and was told that he would only be released once he agreed to pay all the damage caused by his drive. He is expected to be out in 2053.

3

Bjorn Unlucky
Thomas Björn
2003 British Open

Ever know it just isn't going to be your day? That is how Thomas Björn must have felt during the 2003 British Open at Sandwich, Kent. A hugely talented golfer with a drop-dead-gorgeous short game, he took a quadruple-bogey eight on the penultimate hole of his first round after accidentally touching the sand with his club and incurring a two-stroke penalty.

Fighting back from that morale-sapping crisis, he was poised to become Denmark's first-ever Major winner with just three holes remaining in the final round. Leading the field by three strokes with four holes remaining, the 32-year old found a pancake lie after hitting his tee-shot into sand on the short sixteenth. Needing three attempts to get out, he racked up a card-wrecking double-bogey, and it cost him the tournament.

"On the 15th I had one hand on the trophy and I let it go," he said after watching the unknown American Ben Curtis parade the trophy that should have been his. "Obviously I'm disappointed, but I thought I deserved a little bit more than I got."

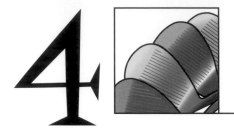

4 Gangster Rap
Machine Gun McGurn
(aka Vince Gebhardi)
Evergreen Golf Club 1933

American mobster Al Capone had a love-hate relationship with golf. While he liked to amuse himself watching his eldest boy Sonny Capone compete in top amateur championships in Florida, his own game was not quite up to the same standard.

Known to carry a loaded pistol in his golf bag, he was shot in the foot after his caddie dropped it on the ground next to him during a round at the Burnham Woods Golf Club in Chicago in 1928!

What happened to the bagman is unknown, but his fate could be no worse than that of Capone henchman, 'Machine Gun' Jack McGurn. A talented golfer who played off a scratch handicap, he entered a number of tournaments, including the prestigious 1933 Western

Open at Olympia Fields Country Club on the outskirts of Chicago.

Playing under the name of Vince Gebhardi, a club pro from nearby Evergreen Golf Club, he was spotted as a fake by a member who had played golf with the real Gebhardi a few weeks earlier and immediately alerted the tournament organisers, who contacted the police, realising they had Public Enemy number five playing in their event.

He was approached by five armed cops on the seventh green, but not wishing to upset him too much, they allowed him to finish his round.

However the news spread like wildfire, and a press photographer began snapping pictures of him putting out on the next hole.

After making a triple bogey, McGurn grabbed him by the neck, and snarled, "You busted up my game, jerk!"

Making an undignified exit, the snapper crawled away with his tail between his legs, 'Machine Gun' finished his game, the police closed in, and they all headed off to jail. Eventually tried and convicted for murder, it is said that he asked for his putter to be buried with him!

5

The Long Drop Club
British Ryder Cup Team
1959

It was a strong Britain and Ireland team that travelled to the USA for the 1959 Ryder Cup at Palm Springs, California. The decision to sail across the Atlantic rather than fly was intended to foster team spirit, but a heavy buffeting in the Atlantic saw many of them violently seasick before the ship had docked in New York.

If they thought their luck was about to change having reached dry land, they were in for another shock. The players climbed on board a twin-engine Convair for a short 40-minute hop from LA to Palm Springs – but with the 1958 Munich air disaster that killed 21 people, including many Manchester United footballers, still fresh in the public's mind, this was one Ryder Cup team that almost never made it.

Flying over the San Jacinto mountain range, they could not avoid the tail end of a hurricane that had devastated parts of Mexico. The turbulence was so violent that an air stewardess was knocked senseless as baggage was tossed around the cabin. Suddenly the plane fell out of the sky, plummeting from 13,000 feet down to 9,000 in a matter of seconds.

A crash seemed inevitable, but the pilot managed to regain control with just seconds to spare. On landing, most passengers fell to their knees and kissed the tarmac in relief. For some years afterwards, the survivors gathered together to relive their experience and were known as the 'Long Drop Club'.

6

A Chip Off the Old Block
Albert 'Sonny' Capone
Chicago circa 1930

Another tale of golfing bad luck from 1930s Gangland Chicago. Albert 'Sonny' Capone had a potentially successful career as a pro golfer ahead of him, but it was cut short through no fault of his own at the age of 27.

Son of the infamous mobster Alfonse Capone – whose main line of work was smuggling in liquor during US prohibition – Sonny was a talented golfer with a low single-figure handicap and he had competed in a number of top amateur tournaments in Florida.

However, he became an obvious target for his father's gangland rivals, and he never went anywhere, including the golf course, without two well-armed bodyguards by his side. Later, when his father was finally locked up for tax evasion, it was thought too dangerous to let Sonny out on his own, with trips to the course the first to be stopped.

Well and Truly Shafted
Thomas Horsburgh
Edinburgh 1894

Possibly the greatest hard luck story in the history of the business side of the game involved a 38-year-old blacksmith from Edinburgh called Thomas Horsburgh. A renowned golfer, he invented the first-ever steel-shafted golf clubs as early as 1894.

Little more than solid steel rods, he even developed a method by which they could be retracted from the wooden club head at will and re-used in another club. Sadly for the blacksmith, he failed to persuade any of the local professionals to commend his revolutionary new idea.

Whether this was out of apathy, or because they saw the new shafts as a threat to their meagre livelihood fitting wooden shafts, we shall never know. What is certain is that, after spending all his money developing the idea, Horsburgh ended up in a Victorian debtors' prison.

8

Partners in Crime
David Gilford
1991 Ryder Cup

At the controversial "War on the Shore" Ryder Cup at Kiawah Island in South Carolina in 1991, world Number One Nick Faldo was surprised to find himself paired with Ryder Cup rookie David Gilford.

Gilford was a shy, unassuming character, and barely a word passed between the two men throughout the entire match. Humiliated 7&6 by Paul Azinger and Mark O'Meara, the British press condemned Faldo for his lack of encouragement and support to the already nervous rookie.

Typically, the winner of four majors to that point brushed off any criticism, stating that he should not have been paired with Gilford in the first place! Writing for a Sunday newspaper, respected golf journalist Lauren St John observed: "Faldo's surliness and Gilford's painful shyness ensured a pairing with less conversation than Trappist monks."

Then, just as Gilford thought his Ryder Cup could not get much worse, an injury to American Steve Pate meant that European Captain Bernard Gallacher was forced to drop one of his own players and concede a half-point to both sides. This meant that the player nominated by the Scot at the beginning of the week had to sit out the singles.

A secret to all but the European captain and his deputies, the name that had been placed in a sealed envelope was David Gilford, and as Gallacher later admitted, "telling David he wasn't playing was one of the toughest things I have ever had to do in my career".

9

Next on the Tee
David Strath
1876 Open. St Andrews.

In 1876, the Open was held at St Andrews for the second time. Unlike the smooth-running event we enjoy today, the organising committee forgot to reserve tee-times for the final two rounds, forcing competitors to slot in between groups of rank amateurs. Tempers began to fray and by the time tournament leader David Strath arrived at the legendary Road Hole, the seventeenth, they had reached boiling point.

Refusing to wait until the green was clear, the unfortunate golfer hit his approach before the green had been cleared, striking the leg of an influential member, who instantly demanded that the tournament organisers disqualify him for 'un-gentlemanly behaviour'.

The following day, Strath turned up on the first tee ready to face fellow professional Bob Martin in a sudden-death play-off, completely unaware that any complaint had been made. Then, just minutes before he was about to tee off, he was informed that the decision to disqualify him would be taken after the result of the play-off was known! Turning on his heels, the St Andrews professional marched off the course complaining that he could not win whatever happened.

Such was the ill feeling that he never played in the Open again. Two years later, he packed his bags for Australia and his luck well and truly ran out when he drowned off the coast of Singapore!

10

Marked For Open Success
Mark Roe
2003 British Open

Mark Roe has a reputation for enjoying life, and that was certainly the case when he found himself right in the thick of things at the 2003 British Open at Sandwich after a brilliant third-round 67. Tied fourth at the time, he was in the form of his life, and looked forward to partnering Tiger Woods in the final round when disaster struck. In one of the biggest sporting disappointments for years, Roe's dream week turned into a nightmare when he was told by playing partner Jesper Parnevik that there was a problem with his scorecard.

It seems they had forgotten to exchange on the first tee and had both signed for their own score, which in the Swede's case was an 81. In typical upbeat style, Roe joked he was distracted by Jesper's bright blue trousers, but the damage was done.

Disqualified from the championship, he headed home to his wife and twin daughters. Roe, 306th in the world and without a tournament win since the 1994 French Open, said he was "dumbfounded and absolutely shell-shocked" as he watched events unfold, glassy-eyed, on television the following day.

And while it was no more than a 'clerical error' that robbed him of the opportunity to win the Claret Jug and a cheque for £700,000, the dignified way he conducted himself in such heartbreaking circumstances won him many fans.

CHAPTER SEVEN

The worst examples of foot in mouth

The worst examples of foot in mouth

Is there a golfer out there who has not shouted out 'great shot!' at the top of his voice, only to watch his partner's ball disappear into a bunker or out of bounds? Worse still are those moments when the mouth engages half a second before the brain, resulting in informing the Lady Captain that 'you hit the ball just like a man!' – perhaps the ultimate faux pas.

Away from the humdrum world of club golfers, one of my favourite examples of Shoe-In-The-Mouth syndrome concerns the great Gary Player. He was playing 'Champagne' Tony Lema in the semi-final of the 1965 Piccadilly World Match Play Championship at Wentworth when he overheard a conversation between two spectators who were following the match.

Five down after 27 holes, defeat was beckoning and the conversation concentrated on whether or not Player could possibly make a comeback. "No chance at all," said one friend to another. "This match is over. Let's go and watch the other one."

One professional who never needed a kick up the backside to play better, Player ambled over to them before openly rebuking both men for writing off his chances. "You obviously don't know anything about golf," he said, "otherwise you should know that a match is never over until the last putt is holed." Quite what they must have thought is unprintable, but Player not only came back to beat Lema – he went on to defeat Peter Thomson in the final. So remember the drill: take up your stance, address the ball, and say absolutely nothing!

1

Fuzzy Faux Pas

Francis Urban Zoeller, or "Fuzzy" to his pals, had long been regarded as one of the more jocular figures on the PGA Tour. That was until he opened his mouth to the press about Tiger Woods in 1997 shortly before he became the first black golfer to win the US Masters at Augusta.

"That little boy is driving well and putting well," commented the former winner. "So, you know what you guys do when he gets in here? You pat him on the back and say congratulations and enjoy it and tell him not to serve fried chicken next year (at the Champions dinner where the reigning champion selects the menu) or collard greens or whatever it is they serve."

Interpreted as a racist comment, an immediate apology was offered by the hapless Zoeller, who said; "It had nothing to do with black, white, purple, yellow or green race. It had nothing to do with Tiger or his family or his golf game. Everyone knows I'm a jokester."

2 Casey Comes a Cropper

Paul Casey could not have imagined the firestorm of criticism he would face after comments he made in a British newspaper in November 2004. A member of the triumphant Ryder Cup team that defeated the USA at Oakland Hills a few months earlier in Detroit, he was quoted as saying how he "properly hates Americans." And this from someone who lives with his American girlfriend in Arizona!

A US tabloid picked up on this howler a few days later, and fuel was added to the fire with the headline: 'Americans are stupid. I hate them!' Hoping to calm things down, the talented young Englishman explained that he was quoted out of context, and that he was only describing the 'winner-take-all' attitude European players had to adopt to beat the Americans at events like the Ryder Cup.

Sadly, it did not help, as he continued to receive death threats on his email and was dropped by one of his equipment sponsors. We can only imagine the welcome he received from US Tour players in the weeks that followed – and with his mind clearly in no fit state, he withdrew from the 2005 US Open after an atrocious first round.

Missing From the Masters

As golfing pundits go, they do not come more straight-talking than American Gary McCord. With his trademark moustache and whiskers, he remains one of the most recognisable figures on the US Tour, but it was working for CBS at the Masters in 1994 that saw him run into trouble with chairman and members of Augusta National – and led to him being gagged.

With strict guidelines on what you can or cannot say during commentary, (like referring to the crowd as "patrons") the flamboyant on course analyst for CBS stretched their patience to the limit by joking, "These greens are so fast, they must be bikini waxed!" Then he described the treacherous slope behind the seventeenth green as, "Where they keep the body bags."

It appears that this was the straw that broke the camel's back. While the members have never admitted they had anything to do with his removal, McCord has not worked at Augusta since.

4 Singh Out of Tune

Vijay Singh has long been known as one of the hardest workers on Tour, but it's unlikely he will get many offers from the diplomatic service after his chauvinistic remarks about ladies' golfer Annika Sorenstam.

In 2003, an invitation was extended to the LPGA star to compete in the Colonial Tournament in May. She became the first woman to play in a men's event in the 45 years since the legendary Babe Zaharias last competed.

The move polarised opinion among a number of top-name golfers, including the world number one. "If I am paired with her, I won't play," said an indignant Singh. "I hope she misses the cut because she doesn't belong out here. This is a men's Tour!"

In the end, the Swedish star did miss the cut by four strokes, but came out of the affair with far more credit than Singh, who attracted a host of uncomplimentary comments.

King of the Carpark
Walter Hagen
Open. Royal Cinque Ports Golf Club. Deal. Kent. July. 1920.

No player brought quite as much colour to the game of golf than Walter Hagen. Eleven-time major winner, the flamboyant American counted Presidents and Kings among his friends and lived by the motto "I never wanted to be a millionaire, I just want to live like one". Possibly the most famous sportsman of his era, imagine the scene when he arrived at Royal Cinque Ports Golf Club on England's south coast to play a practice round prior to the 1920 Open. Heading for the clubhouse to change into his spikes, he was stopped at the door by the secretary who told him in no uncertain terms that professionals were not allowed inside and that he would have to use the caddie shed like the rest of the competitors! Not surprisingly, the 'Haig' was incensed by the snub and made his displeasure obvious by turning up each day in a chauffeur-driven Rolls Royce. Parking it in full view of the members, he would change his shoes in the back, then after each round, ate cucumber sandwiches and sipped champagne from the large Fortnum and Mason hamper he had delivered specially each day. As for the Golf Club, was it really a coincidence they were never invited to host another Open?

6 The US Ryder Cup Food Aid Programme

Ganton. Yorkshire. England.
16-17 September 1949

Arriving in Southampton for the first Ryder Cup match played on British soil for twelve years, the United States team ran straight into a storm of controversy.

Robert Hudson, the American industrialist and team manager, had taken the unusual step of transporting $1,300-worth of fresh meat over to England. An easy-going individual, Hudson explained to the awaiting press that with food rationing still in force, the cost of feeding the American squad would be spared their British hosts by bringing in their own food.

Unaware of the storm of controversy that his words caused, he then dug himself in even deeper after expressing his sincere hope that the British players would help them eat through a haul which included six hundred steaks, twelve sides of rib-eye beef for roasting, a dozen hams, and twelve boxes of smoked bacon!

Smacking of charity, the controversial fare was later served at an American-sponsored banquet for the two teams in London. On finding out, the wives of British team members all refused to take part – unlike their husbands, who appear to have tucked in heartily.

7

Monty has the Yanks in a Funk

Colin Montgomerie attracts controversy like some Hollywood film stars attract paternity suits. In the run-up to the 1997 Ryder Cup at Valderrama, he was forced to write to US Captain Tom Kite and individual members of the team concerning comments he had made about PGA Tour star, Brad Faxon. With talk of other US Tour players cold-shouldering him on his next visit to the States, the Scot was quoted as saying that Faxon "is going through a divorce and mentally I don't think he will be with it."

Igniting a firestorm of indignation across the Atlantic, Fred Funk responded by telling *American Golf Week* magazine: "He is the jerk of the world as far as I'm concerned and you can write that down because when I see him I'm going to tell him to his face."

The usually mild-mannered Loren Roberts summed up the feelings of many of his fellow players when he said: "Taking shots at a guy's personal life is a little too much."

Regarding future trips to American tournaments, Bob Estes added: "Who's Monty going to play practice rounds with? I always knew he was a cry-baby. I respect his skills, but when he starts with the low blows… that's poor."

8

Jones Jumps Ship

Like haggis, neeps and tatties, the Old Course
at St Andrews is an acquired taste but once it
has you under its spell, it never lets go.
If you are still in any doubt, consider the legendary
Grand Slam winner, Robert T. Jones Junior, who made
his Open Championship debut here as a fiery 19-year-
old in 1921.

Contradicting his future reputation for fair play
and limitless self-control, he was going along steadily
in the third round when he failed to extract himself

from a steep-faced greenside bunker on the short par 3 eleventh hole. Running up a score of 8, he tore up his scorecard and stamped off the golf course in an absolute rage. "At no place but St Andrews," he fumed, "would these hazards be acceptable, but on the Old Course they are as acceptable as the grey stone of the houses that line the closing hole."

Six years later in 1927, Bobby returned to the Kingdom of Fife to record the second of his three Open victories. Sparking a lifetime affection for the links, the town and its citizens, he was given the freedom of St Andrews in 1952, where he spoke the immortal words: "If I had to play one golf course for the rest of my life it would be the Old Course at St Andrews."

9

Mauled by the Golden Bear

One golf journalist suffered every writer's nightmare when he wrote, on the eve of the 1986 US Masters at Augusta, that Jack Nicklaus was all washed up and that he had zero chance of winning. So imagine his horror when the legendary Golden Bear raced through the field on the final day to become the oldest winner in the tournament's history!

Tom McCollister was a respected sportswriter with The *Atlanta Journal-Constitution* who had covered the Masters for many years. Rating the competitors in terms of possible winners, top-ten finishers and total outsiders, he came to Nicklaus.

"I just thought he hadn't played well all that year, or the year before," he admitted later. "So, I just wrote that he's done. He's gone. His clubs are rusty. It was just a big paragraph, really."

John Montgomery, a close friend of Nicklaus, saw the article, and knew how mad it would make him when he read it. But rather than just hand it over, he pasted it up on the refrigerator door in the Augusta house that Jack was renting that week with his family. Reading it every morning over his orange juice and muffins, it obviously had the desired effect, because Nicklaus went on to win the tournament – then credited the McCollister article for providing the incentive.

10 A Calculated Error of Judgement

Like John Wayne and John F. Kennedy, some American cultural icons are just beyond criticism. If you need proof, ask former Open champion Mark Calcavecchia, who took an ill-advised pot-shot at the legendary Arnold Palmer prior to the 2004 US Masters at Augusta.

To the consternation of the golfing world, the 1989 Open champ urged him to call it a day saying, "Arnold still loves to play golf, but there's no point being out there if you shoot 83–84. You have to end it, don't you?"

Not surprisingly, the moment he saw it in print, the 38-year-old American Ryder Cup professional instantly regretted telling one of the game's greatest-ever players to quit: "I should never have opened my mouth," he said, scoffing down humble pie quicker than John Daly eats hamburgers. "I was out of line saying what I did," he admitted later. "I will learn from it because I had no right to say it. We're talking about Arnold Palmer here."

He had to write a letter of apology to the great man, which it is understood was graciously accepted. There is no truth in the rumour that Calc intends to join the diplomatic corps after his career in golf comes to an end.

CHAPTER EIGHT

The worst challenges

The worst challenges

With estimated odds of 25,000–1 against the average hacker scoring a hole-in-one, you might think hitting one is as rare as a final-day Tiger Woods collapse. Harry Vardon, who only scored one in his lifetime, once described it as 'the perfect fluke', and that was the perception for many years. Many more describe it as pure luck.

That was until two enterprising punters from the North of England discovered that, far from being extreme rarities, holes-in-one were a fairly regular occurrence at professional tournaments. In fact, they averaged around one a week on the European Tour, with even more on the PGA Tour in America, where four were recorded at the 1989 US Open alone!

Consequently, a large number of bets were placed with bookmakers, at odds of between 10–1 and 150–1, that a hole-in-one would be scored at three British tournaments in 1991 – the Benson and Hedges International, The Volvo PGA, and the Open. Guess what? Each tournament produced an ace, and they pocketed a small fortune before the mean-spirited bookies slashed the odds all over the country to less than evens.

It was a betting coup in the purest sense, and for those of us who have lost money betting on the half-time score at Old Trafford or the number of runs scored in an innings at Lord's, the news brought a real smile to our collective faces. The only problem as golfers was: why did we not think of it first?

Like the two intrepid gamblers, this chapter is all about people trying to part someone else from their hard-earned cash. The only difference is they attempted it on the golf course, not off it, but the results, as you will discover, were surprisingly similar.

1

I'd Put my Life on it
Sir David Moncreiffe
St Andrews 1870

The urge to bet that you can play a hole in fewer strokes than your partner has proved irresistible to all of us at one time or another. However, back in 1870, the records of the Royal and Ancient Golf Club of St. Andrews tell of one wager in which Sir David Moncreiffe bet his life against that of John Whyte-Melville, with the eventual winner presenting a new silver golf club to the members.

Today, the record books omit to tell us who actually won the match, but thirteen years after the match was played, John Whyte-Melville gave a speech where he expressed his deep regret at the death of Sir David Moncreiffe, and perhaps more significantly "the causes that led to it".

Dressed to Win

John Farrar
Royston 1914

As if to prove showman Phineas T. Barnum's famous saying, "there's one sucker born every minute", an unusual bet was offered to the members of Royston Golf Club in 1914. Member John Farrar boasted he could go round the southern course in less than 100 strokes wearing full army kit issue.

An army officer, and obviously therefore accustomed to wearing the heavy gear, he offered odds of 10–1, and took a small fortune in bets. Two hours later, the round was over and he had won his bet. He then offered a challenge to a local golf professional, who failed to break 100... and Farrar took even more money.

Perhaps he could have got better odds if he had offered to play in the same outfit as Harry De'ath a few years later. A leading opera singer, he played an inter-club match wearing a full suit of armour.

3

Measuring up to the Challenge
Harry Rowntree
Littlehampton 1924

Showing that anything is possible in golf, amateur golfer Harry Rowntree wagered he could beat two former Open winners, starting on level scores, and win!

Receiving an overall 'allowance' of 150 yards, he beat Edward Ray and George Duncan by the amazing score of 6&5. Able to pick his ball up at any time, he made a 'hole-in-one' on a par 3… where he 'walked' the ball into the cup after hitting his tee-shot into a greenside bunker!

When in a ditch, he was able to lift and drop for no penalty, and when out-of-bounds he simply walked it back onto the fairway. For the loss of a few inches, he could improve his lie immeasurably. And for the loss of a few more, he could hole every putt he ever attempted. Ray commented afterwards that if he had a 'gimme' of one yard per round he would win every tournament he ever played in.

4 Dropping in for a Game

New York 1928 and Sonning 1931

An intrepid group of American golfers thought it would be fun to drop balls from an aeroplane onto Westbury Golf Club in New York in 1928. First wrapping the balls in cloth so they did not bounce, they placed bets on who would finish closest to each hole, with a score-keeper on the ground to mark their cards. Nobody knows whether the course was closed at the time or not, but the record books show the match was won three-up by the team captained by a William Hammond.

Three years later, Captain Pennington of the Royal Air Force took part in a similar match at Sonning Golf Club near Reading. Competing against the more conventionally-obtained score of Club Professional Arthur Young down on the ground, he took 80 balls up in his plane, and dropped them onto the green via his bomb hatch!

Exactly how the scoring worked is unsure, as is his method for repairing pitch-marks, but the record books show that he went round in 29 strokes compared to his rival's highly creditable 68.

5 Blackballed at Hoylake

1912 Hoylake

John Ball jnr, winner of both the Open and British Amateur Championships, bet a group of members that he could play Royal Liverpool in under 90 strokes, inside three hours and without losing a ball… the problem being that it was blanketed in a thick sea fog at the time!

Using a ball he had painted black especially for such an occasion, the sun broke through halfway round and cleared the mist. Taking full advantage, the legendary golfer went round in 81 in just over two hours, and won his bet.

Twenty years later, Hoylake, home to the 2006 Open, was the venue for other unusual wager. Played off level between a scratch player and a six-handicapper, the latter had the right to shout "boo!" three times during the game. With a small fortune riding on the result, the cunning golfer saved up his 'advantage' until the thirteenth hole, where he used up his first "boo!" The scratch player was so distracted waiting for the next two shouts that he lost his nerve and the match. Some golfers may have heard a far cruder version of this story – but this is how it began!

6 Singing for His Supper
Original forms of handicapping

In 1927, Opera singing star Orville Harold and lawyer John Walsh played an unusual match at the Wee Burn Country Club in Darien, Connecticut. Betting $200 on the outcome, the singer was allowed two high C's during the match to compensate for his opponent's lower handicap. Unfortunately any hope he had that it would break his concentration was lost when Mr Walsh secretly wore earplugs throughout the entire match. On the same theme, the Addington Golf Club in the south of England was the home to yet another curious wager in 1952. This time between a scratch player and high handicap golfer, the bet was that the scratch man was required to drink a large whisky and soda on every tee starting at the first. Playing off level, they both made it to the 16th tee, where the scratch player collapsed in a drunken heap and forfeited the match – a game he was leading one-up at the time.

7 Kept in the Dark
18th-century Scotland

With bare-knuckle fights, cock fighting and bear baiting popular pastimes in the second half of the 19th century, the upper classes in Scotland also enjoyed wagering serious sums on a game of golf. Concerned at the amount of high-stakes gambling going on, the Honourable Company of Edinburgh Golfers at Musselburgh capped the amount one member could win from another in a day's play back in 1766. It seemed that too many duels were being fought to settle their on-course disputes, but the ruling did not allow for the ingenuity of these golfing gamblers who soon found a way around it With the limit set on how much you could win in one day's play, matches were played over three holes at night with the caddies holding a lantern to show the way! Taking a more practical attitude, the Society of St. Andrews Golfers, turned a blind eye to their members' excesses, realising that no one would play golf if they tried to ban on-course gambling! But even they finally lost patience in November 1822 after one of the members used the committee minute book to record his bets!

8

Four!
Ben Sayers
Edinburgh 1910

In the past, large sums have been bet on golfers versus archers matches, golfers against fly fishermen and – most remarkably of all – a match involving the legendary Harry Vardon and a javelin champion!

Another famous golfing gambler around the turn of the last century was the renowned Scottish professional, Ben Sayers. Standing just 5' 3" tall, he was a tough competitor who was unlucky not to win the Open on a number of occasions.

A successful businessman, he made a small

fortune selling clubs and balls from his shop on the West Links at North Berwick, along with a number of course-design commissions. Known as a gruff individual, he also had the reputation of not suffering fools gladly.

On one legendary occasion in 1910, he was challenged by an American visitor to Royal Burgess Golf Club in Edinburgh, who foolishly questioned his claim that he could play every hole in a score of 4! Not someone given to idle boasting, Sayers grabbed a set of clubs, and headed to the first tee, followed by an interested crowd of onlookers. Putting together a round of incredible consistency, he made 4 at every par 3, every par 4, and most significantly, every par 5 hole, recording a total of 72 strokes!

9

Masking Your Real Talent

William Horne
New York, 1912

Like all stereotypes, the golfing bandit has long since had his day. The time when a professional standard player like Lee Trevino or Chi Chi Rodriguez could turn up unannounced at a posh Golf Club and part the member with the lowest handicap from his money is no longer possible. But that was definitely not the case in New York in 1912. Appearing out of nowhere, a masked golfer with a cut-glass British accent issued a big-money $1,000 challenge against any American golfer who thought they could beat him. Never appearing in public without his disguise mask or painting his face black, he practised in front of huge crowds, who were duly impressed with the prodigious hitting of this talented stranger. Having eliminated legendary British golfers Harry Vardon and James Braid from the search via a telegram to their respective Golf Clubs in England, the mystery deepened. Indeed, so strong was the interest that news reporters camped outside his hotel hoping to uncover his identity but no one accepted the wager until US Open Champion Johnny McDermott stepped into the breach.

"McDermott has accepted the Black Mask's challenge," boasted *Golf Illustrated* magazine in October. "…the contest will take place this month and for the first time in history since the days of chivalry, the champion will meet a masked unknown …"

Sadly the report was premature. McDermott 'would' play the masked golfer but felt that such a match would "demean the honourable and dignified nature of the sport." Of course, if he wanted to play without any disguise he would be happy to take him on. The editor of *American Golfer* magazine agreed saying, "Our courses are not three-ringed circus tents and our players are not in the habit of appearing in the character of a buffoon. Wash your face man and come clean …"

Eventually, he did come clean. Exposed by the *Daily Mirror* a few weeks later, William Horne, a surprisingly little-known professional at Laleham Golf Club in Chertsey, admitted to being the masked golfer.

10

A Real Hammering
Titanic Thomson
Tucson 1948

Sam Snead, Gene Sarazen and Byron Nelson, he beat them all – yet you will never find the name of Titanic Thomson in the golfing record books. Probably the most naturally gifted golfer of his era, he preferred to spend his time "plucking pigeons" on the golf courses of Arizona and California during the late forties and early fifties.

More golf sting than golf swing, Titanic would skin his man on the gaming tables, then again on the golf course the next day – having played a few holes badly to persuade them to up the ante.

One group of high rollers took up his challenge to play a round of golf using nothing but a household hammer. Played at El Rio Resort, Tucson, each of the seven players stumped up $1000 on the basis that none of them had a clue how to hit the ball. Sadly, what they did not know was that Thomson had been practising for the past three weeks and had already shot level par! Grabbing the money and running, a contract was put out on his life by at least one of the cheated golfers, but it failed to deter this inveterate gambler – the next time he tried it, he used a broom!

CHAPTER NINE

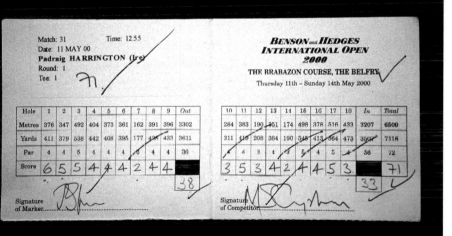

The worst rule breakers

The worst rule-breakers

Henry Longhurst once commented that the rules of golf should cover no more space than the back of a matchbox. His fellow golfing scribe Horace Hutchinson would probably agree with him, having once accused a fellow golfer of bending the rules during an important match at Royal Liverpool in 1912.

His opponent had the bad luck to find his ball resting in a rabbit hole, but to his frustration, it was just out of arm's reach. The ball had to be identified to declare it lost, but this was just not possible as the make and number were lying the wrong way round!

"That is a lost ball, then," declared Hutchinson, to his fellow golfer's disgust.

"Lost ball?" he retorted.

"How can it be lost when I can see the damn thing?"

"I say the ball is lost unless you can gather it up and hold it in your hand," said Horace, before marching off down the fairway with barely a backward glance.

Narrowly losing his match, the incident was immediately referred to the tournament organisers, who, not surprisingly, ruled in favour of their fellow committee member, Hutchinson. Resigning from the Club in disgust, his foe maintained that he would never play the course again until he had 'trained a ferret to draw out golf balls'.

Some of the golfers included in this chapter must have felt pretty much the same.

1

Locking up Victory
Bobby Locke
1957 Open, St Andrews

The first televised Open in 1957 also proved to be the one of the most controversial. Bobby Locke of South Africa holed out on the final green at St Andrews to win his fourth title, thwarting Peter Thomson's attempt to add to the five he ended up with.

Amazingly, a sharp-eyed viewer noticed that Locke had failed to replace his ball after moving it off the line of his playing opponent. It was only a matter of inches, but as the Championship committee ruled afterwards, it would have not have affected the result as the infringement incurred a two-shot penalty, and he won by three.

What is certain is that golf's modern-day ruling body would not have been quite as liberal in their interpretation of the incident as the predecessors: "Whether we could justifiably reach the same conclusion today is a different matter," said R&A Rules Chairman, David Rickman. In simple terms, Locke would have been disqualified for signing an incorrect scorecard.

2 The Road to Success?
Bob Gaared
Los Angeles Golf Club 1950

Playing in a club competition at Los Angeles Golf Club, Bob Gaared sliced his drive out of bounds on the 425-yard, par-4 second. The ball bounced off a tarmac road and into a passing truck. The driver hearing the noise stopped his vehicle next to the green.

Having no idea of the rules of golf, he signalled that he had found the ball and placed it in the hole for safekeeping. Gaared convinced himself that he had made a one and entered it on his scorecard. Unfortunately, his club committee disagreed and disqualified him for not having declared his first ball out-of-bounds. He should have penalised himself two strokes.

Surprisingly, even if Mr Gaared's mammoth effort had counted, it would still not have been the 'longest' ace in history. That record goes to amateur Robert Mitera for his effort at the downhill 447-yard tenth hole, at the appropriately named Miracle Hills GC in Omaha.

3 Grooving Away with the Prize

Jock Hutchison
1921 Open

Winning the Open is a life-long dream for many of the world's top golfers, but winning it at St Andrews is considered something really special. Yet not all winners have been honoured in quite the same way as the expatriated US-domiciled Scot, Jock Hutchison, following his controversial victory in 1921.

In conditions more akin to the Sahara than St Andrews, he defeated top English amateur Roger Wethered by nine strokes in the 36-hole play-off, but it was his uncanny ability to hold his approach shots on the rock-hard greens that was the talk of St Andrews.

It seemed that he had used a set of heavily-grooved 'Bakspin' irons throughout the week. Declared illegal soon afterwards, his use of them had brought scowls of disapproval from the golfing press, and there was even the odd shout of "cheat" at the presentation ceremony.

Heading back to New York with the silver Claret Jug in his suitcase and his tail between his legs, Hutchison was forever tainted by the accusation that he "bought the Open for the price of a set of clubs."

4

Can I Have my Ball Back Please?
Raymond Russell
2001 English Open

Scottish World Cup professional Raymond Russell had high hopes of a top-ten position going into the last round of the Compass English Open at the Forest of Arden in 2001. However, these hopes were ruined at the 12th green when he inexplicably threw his ball into a greenside water hazard!

Of course, he meant to throw it to the caddie for cleaning, but he took his eye off the ball, and was forced to watch in horror as it rolled into the aqua and disappeared forever. Sending his bagman wading into the murky depths, the result was a lost ball, followed by a two-stroke penalty and almost £4,500 in prize money!

5

Pyramid Problems
Gary Player
Egypt 1955

Often the most broken rules in golf are the local ones established by each course. Hoping to account for every possible contingency from landing next to artificial poles for electric wires to being attacked by wild animals, they can often make fascinating reading. The legendary Gary Player was competing in the Egyptian Match Play Championship in 1955 when his drive on the final hole came to rest against a stone wall. Considered an immovable obstruction, the South African was forced "to play it as it lay" Typically, his next shot ricocheted off it and knocked him out stone cold. Recovering long enough to finish out, he was then penalised two shots for having been struck by the ball and lost the match. Not unlike former US president George Bush who pole-axed his former vice-president Dan Quayle after a wayward drive struck him on the head during the Doug Sanders Celebrity Classic in Texas.

6  Snakes Alive
Singapore 1972.

Scottish professional Jimmy Stewart was competing in the Singapore Open in 1972 when his ball caught the attention of a King Cobra that mistook it for an egg. Bravely dispatching the large snake with one blow of his iron he was amazed to see another, smaller snake wriggle out from its mouth. Repeating the exercise, Stewart went on to finish his round, but not before someone accused him of breaking the rule concerning what you can and cannot do to improve your lie! Referring the incident to the ruling body of golf – The Royal and Ancient Golf Club of St Andrews – it was decided that under the circumstances, he should not be penalised for improving his lie! Some years later, another pro was playing at Yaoundé in Cameroon in 1985 when a snake wriggled between his legs. With barely a thought he altered the angle of his down swing and killed the reptile with a single blow. The question then arose whether this was deemed a stroke or not? Referring the matter to the ultimate authority it was ruled that the action of "transforming the snake from an outside agency to a loose impediment" was fully justified under the circumstances and subsequently there would be no two-shot penalty.

7

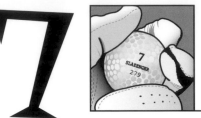

Irish Eyes Were Not Smiling
Padraig Harrington
The Belfry 2000

Few players can boast to have represented their region at both Walker Cup and Ryder Cup levels. One such player is the genial Irishman Padraig Harrington. Registering tournament victories in both Europe and the United States, along with over $5 million in prize money, this top ranking golfer now has his eyes set on a major victory that will seal his rapid rise to fame and fortune. Amazingly it was not always the case. Turning professional in 1997, he expressed his simple desire just to "earn a decent living" from the game he loved. So when he found himself five strokes clear going into the final round of the Benson and Hedges International Open at the Belfry back in 2000, it must have seemed like a dream come true. With the prospect of winning one of European Golf's flagship events, he must have wondered if he had walked under a ladder or broken his hotel mirror when it was discovered that he had forgotten to sign his first-round scorecard. Like all scorecard infringements, the penalty was disqualification and despite a huge fuss in the media to change the rules, the Dubliner headed home a wiser but poorer man.

8 Watson Rules

It used to be said in Scotland that if a player shouted "fore" three times before hitting his tee-shot, then no court in the land would convict him of manslaughter should he be unfortunate enough to kill someone with his ball! Perhaps the same principle held true for five-time Open winner, Tom Watson. A hugely popular golfer north of the border, he conducted himself with charm and sportsmanship on his many visits to the Home of Golf. So when the clubs he used to win the 1975 Open, 1977 United States PGA Championship and 1977 Open were deemed not to conform to strict R&A and USGA rules and regulations some years later, it was unthinkable that his titles would be expunged from the record books. And so it proved. Ruling that no significant advantage was sought or gained, his record was allowed to stand.

CHAPTER TEN

The worst dressed golfers

153

The worst-dressed golfers

Admit it – golf has long been known as a sport for the fashionably challenged. Ask most non-golfers about on-course clothing, and they will talk about 'Rupert Bear' check trousers, garishly-coloured shirts, and diamond-patterned woollen jumpers from Scotland.

Certainly this was the case for many years, but with the emergence of Tiger Woods for the men and Michelle Wie for the girls, the media tell us that this is no longer true. Golf, they say, is the new polo, where on-course style translates easily into night-club chic, where slipovers are essential day-wear, and turtleneck jumpers are an absolute necessity when it comes to that all-important business meeting.

But those golfers among you who have been elevated effortlessly from fashion victim to style icon in the space of a few short years, beware the capricious nature of high couture. As this chapter reveals, the Royal and Ancient Game came rock-bottom of the style list for decades, and with the help of many of those listed, is destined to head straight back from whence it came...

1

Dressed to Thrill

Ian Poulter

A golfing maverick in the mould of Max Faulkner and Doug Sanders, Ian Poulter has a taste for garish clothing, as anyone who saw him competing in the 2004 Open at Royal Troon would no doubt testify.

Dressed in red, white and blue 'Union Jack' trousers one day and tartan plus-fours with pink knee-length socks the next, this is one golfer who likes attention. Add in the spiked hair flecked with the colour of his favourite football team (red for Arsenal), and you start to get the picture.

This, however, was no impulse fashion disaster, as a phone call to Beck Tailoring in Bellevue, Washington clearly shows. Receiving an order for eight pairs of plus-fours – or knickers, as they are known in the USA – they were surprised to hear a young English voice on the phone. The customer, as it turned out, was Ryder Cup star Poulter, and the only stipulation he made was that they had to be delivered to Britain in time for the Open a few weeks later.

The rest as they say, is history – and his garb on the first day of the Open a year later followed suit. Sadly, the claret jug he sported on his strides was the only one he got close to all week.

2

Suits you Sir

Max Faulkner

'**M**ad' Max Faukner brought a much-needed dash of colour to drab post-war Britain of the forties and fifties. An engaging mixture of Hollywood good looks, confidence and sublime golfing ability, Max Faulkner was an Open champion when home-grown winners were rarer than John Daly diet tips or Tiger Woods off-days. Competitive to his fingertips, he was someone who never did anything by halves. Typical of someone who put Marine Commandos through their paces during World War II, he would entertain the crowds by walking down the fairway on his hands or by hitting shots blindfolded! Then if the action really slowed he began giving impromptu lessons to astonished but appreciative onlookers. As for legendary figures like Hogan and Snead, he took them on and beat them both. Among the first British players to play regularly in the United States, he even threatened to punch Slammin' Sam's lights out when he once accused him of gamesmanship!

He was also a showman. At a time when sombre browns and greys were the norm among golf professionals he marched to victory at the 1951 Open Championship at Royal Portrush dressed in a bright blue shirt, canary yellow plus-fours and matching shoes and socks! Even in his eighties, he would play golf in a red polo-necked shirt and purple trousers and rarely failed to beat his age right up until his death in 2005.

3  Get ahead, Get a Hat
Jesper Parnevik

In an age of uniform swings, uniform clothing and uniform utterances to the press, one Swedish professional, Jesper Parnevik, stands out from the crowd. Famed for eating volcanic dust to improve his digestion, this pencil-slim golfer is equally well known for his figure-hugging trousers and taste for outlandish golf shirts. He has come close on numerous occasions, most notably at the Open at Turnberry in 1997, to winning the major championship that would cap a hugely successful career. An inveterate cigar smoker, he pulls one out every time he arrives at the final hole of a tournament he is about to win. Yet it is headgear that this maverick Ryder Cup pro is most famous for. The first player to sport a baseball cap with the peak pulled back, this is one fashion statement that came about purely by accident. Ragged by his golfing chums for having a pure white forehead, he decided to flip his cap back like a latter-day Norman Wisdom and complete his tan. Attracting all sorts of strange looks, Parnevik had the last laugh as sponsors lined up to advertise on the underside of the peak.

4 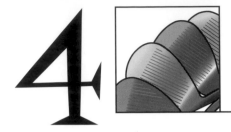 No Payne, No Gain
Payne Stewart

US Open champion Payne Stewart was a larger-than-life character whose outlandish taste in clothing reflected his personality.

Rarely seen in anything but his trademark plus-fours and woollen socks, he signed a lucrative sponsorship deal with the National Football League back in the mid-1990s, and from then on wore the team colours of every American Football franchise.

Set off by silver-tipped golf shoes, he picked up the idea after watching Australian Rodger Davis playing a tournament in Europe in 1980. Stylish and flamboyant, the Twenties Look became his trademark, and after he died in a tragic plane crash back in 2000, players and officials all sported plus-fours at a memorial service held in his honour.

5

Oh Dear O'Leary
John O'Leary

Irish professional John O'Leary **must wince every time he sees a photograph of himself from the** 1970s. A regular on the European tournament scene, he put the 'eck into check trousers. No bright colours or bizarre designs were out of bounds for the sartorially-challenged Ryder Cup golfer.

Flower power had nothing to do with it, as he sported every imaginable design from dandelions to diamonds, plaid to stripes. And if that was not enough, he added to the overall effect with a frizzy Afro haircut and designer stubble!

By way of contrast, John now spends most of his working life in a smart jacket and tie as representative of the European Tour.

The Rook's Rest
Smelly Bob Andrew

Today, the British Open is among the most prestigious tournaments on the golfing calendar, with smartly turned out professionals all sporting their blue-chip sponsor's logos on their bag and clothing. It was certainly not the case back in November 1860, when the first championship was played at Prestwick Golf Club. With the Ayrshire coast proving a long and difficult journey from Edinburgh and St Andrews, it attracted an entry of just eight professionals, including home favourite Tom Morris and Musselburgh's great champion and the eventual winner, William Park. Entries were also accepted from Andrew Strath, Charles Hunter, Alexander Smith,

William Steel and one particularly strange individual named Bob Andrew. Little more than a vagrant, he worked as a caddy in St Andrews and was nicknamed 'The Rook' because he never washed and his face was as black as a crow's feathers. Nonetheless he was a talented golfer and his entry was accepted. Unfortunately one look at him by the tournament organisers threw them into a panic. With holes in shoes, tobacco stains on his shirt and a week's growth of beard, it was thought that he would frighten the ladies who might wish to follow the action. And he was not the only scruffy golfer on display that week! Stepping into the breach, the Earl of Eglington, one of the event sponsors, immediately sent for eight 'golfing suits' in his own tartan to dress each competitor in. A generous gesture, it also proved a useful aid to identifying Andrew after he was thrown into jail on a charge of drunk and disorderly, the night before the competition was due to begin...

7  Ryder Cup Rebels

Englishmen Ken Brown and Mark James were newcomers to the Ryder Cup in September 1979. With the luxurious Greenbrier Golf Club in West Virginia, scheduled to host the first-ever match between the USA and a combined European team, their alarmingly casual dress prior to the match mirrored their attitude throughout the entire week, according to team captain, John Jacobs. At Heathrow Airport, Jacobs struggled to control the independently-minded young men. While the rest of their team-mates turned up smartly attired in the official team uniform, Brown and James chose to travel to America in more casual dress – with Brown, in the words of captain Jacobs looking 'terrible'. It was the start of what was going to be a difficult week between the three men. The problems extended to the opening flag ceremony where both professionals, vexed at having to wear the official team uniform, displayed a frankly disinterested attitude. They were also disciplined for strolling through the shops when they should have attended a team meeting called by John Jacobs. In spite of calls to leave them out altogether, Jacobs steadfastly refused, feeling that their excess energy was better put to use against the Americans. It proved to be a mistake – James, who was carrying a chest muscle injury, played poorly and the British pair lost by 3 and 2 in their match against Trevino and Zeoller. That said, Brown won his singles match against Zoeller, which only seemed to make matters worse. "The fact that Ken Brown, pursuing his young, idiosyncratic way, was eventually one of only three British and European winners in the singles," wrote respected columnist Laddie Lucas, "only compounded the wretchedness of the whole affair." Showing how time cures all ills, both men are now among the most highly respected figures in European Golf and leading broadcasters for the BBC.

8

Waldorf Salad with Extra Nuts
Duffy Waldorf

Big-hitting American professional **Duffy Waldorf spends most of his working life dressed like the** worst kind of day-tripping tourist. Sporting a wide range of garish Hawaiian golf shirts, one fellow player thought his gear looked like "he had just survived an explosion in a paint factory!"

But Duffy remains immune to the criticism. He says that his shirts remind him of home when he is out on the PGA Tour. "When I'm home I wear exactly this type of shirt," he admitted. "That's my lifestyle and I figure that it's important not to take yourself so seriously. After all, golf is just a game."

9  The Iceman Cometh

David Duval was never the most outgoing of professionals. Famed for wearing wrap-around dark shades before, during and after a round of golf, they added to his unemotional, iceman image.

Winner of the 2001 Open at Royal Lytham, he conducted pre-tournament interviews in his shades, even when indoors in the press centre. Indeed, the only time the golfing public got to see his eyes was at the presentation ceremony, when the American star finally took them off to receive the Silver Claret jug!

Some thought it was the affectation of a painfully private individual, but the explanation was simpler than that. It seemed that he had a lifelong allergy to dust and pollen, and the glasses helped prevent his eyes from watering.

CHAPTER ELEVEN

The rest of the worst

The rest of the worst

In every book that deals with stories from the wonderful world of golf there are always a few that simply do not fit. You include them because they illustrate a theme or highlight a point but like a square golf ball in a round hole, they stand out like a sore thumb when the final selection is arrived at. Now you have a dilemma. They are fascinating stories, and you want the reader to be amazed by your taste in selecting them, but where to put them? Then comes a moment of inspiration. Your clever editor suggests an extra chapter dealing with all these waifs and strays and your problem is solved.

Hence this chapter. Enjoy.

1 A Dream Round That Turned into a Nightmare

Think about this next time you sneak out the house on Sunday morning for a quick round of golf! In February 1610, the Kirk Sessions at St Andrews banned the playing of golf on the Sabbath. A fixed tariff of charges was set, with a fine of 10 shillings for a first offence, rising to 20 shillings for the second and a spell in the stocks for "publick repentance" for the third.

Draconian as these punishments were, it was known that some clergy-men played golf, including the Bishop of Galloway, who had a terrible vision of two men attacking him on Leith Links in 1619! A keen golfer, he obviously had an attack of conscience, as this vision came just days after he had accepted the venerable position of Bishop after initially denying that he would. Knowing he had broken church law by playing golf, he was racked with guilt. He then threw down his clubs, took to his bed – and died soon after.

2 The Ultimate Explosion Shot

Ever wondered what happened to the banana that you left in your golf bag weeks ago? Well, now you have something else to worry about. A book entitled "Nuclear Terrorism: The Ultimate Preventable Catastrophe" was published in 2004, and included a section on the many ways a terrorist might deliver a nuclear bomb within striking distance of the world's major cities – including shipping one in a bag of golf clubs via a package delivery service!

Written by Graham Allison, founding dean of Harvard's Kennedy School of Government and director of Harvard's Belfer Center for Science and International Affairs, it is guaranteed to put the wind up any golfer who hears a ticking sound coming from inside the ball pocket. But they needn't have worried; as every hacker knows, virtually nothing that comes out of a golf bag ever works the way it is meant to.

3

Open Wide
Before You Tee Off

Taking the day off in the hope of qualifying for the U.S Seniors Open at Crestwood C.C., Massachusetts, Rhode Island peridontist Dr George Pirie thought the 69 he shot in the sectional heats would not be good enough, so he drove straight back to his surgery.

Rescheduling his appointments, he performed oral surgery on three patients while he waited for play to conclude. In between, he tried to telephone the organisers, but without success. Deciding to cancel his last two appointments, he headed back to the course, where to his surprise, he found himself in a three-man play-off with Paul Parajeckas and Paul Quigley, brother of established Champions Tour player Brett.

With only two spots available, Pirie, 54, barely had time to hit some practice balls before he was shuttled out to the first sudden-death hole. Catching his breath, he managed to hole a 12-foot birdie putt to book his place at Bellerive C.C. in St Louis – his first-ever major championship. Let's hope it wasn't a case of feeling down in the mouth when he didn't win.

4 A Right Charlie

Desperate to get the professional game under way as quickly as possible after the end of World War II, the British Professional Golfers' Association organised five tournaments in 1945. The most significant was The Daily Mail Victory Tournament at St. Andrews, which attracted 172 entrants, including American star Lloyd Mangrum, who turned up in uniform. Often called the 'unofficial' or 'lost' Open, it was won by RAF crewman Charles H. Ward who, amazingly, was confined to barracks after returning to his RAF camp at Wallingfold a day late because the presentation made him miss his train!

5 Wide Open Borders

The Open has been played since 1860, and is the oldest of the four major golf championships. With pre-qualifying events introduced into America, Australia and South Africa in recent years, it is run under the auspices of the Royal and Ancient Golf Club of St Andrews, and has a well-deserved reputation for being superbly organised.

But in the run-up to the 2002 Open at Muirfield, there was a small blip, as it launched an investigation after 47 out of 48 Nigerians who were granted visas to enter Britain to take part in the pre-qualifying event failed to turn up! Nigeria has no particular reputation for golfing prowess, and the alarm bells should have been ringing long before their applications were processed.

Speaking later, the immigration service confirmed there were strong suspicions that some of the would-be golfers had no intention of taking part in the tournament, but used the event as an excuse to get past passport controls. Oh really?

6 Trophy Trouble

You expect it in rugby, but definitely not the genteel game of golf. A few years ago, the famous Calcutta Cup was kicked around an Edinburgh street by international rugby players, but it comes as quite a shock to find the near-priceless Ryder Cup damaged during post-match celebrations.

Purchased in 1926 for £200, and donated to the PGA by Samuel Ryder a year later, the foot-high golden trophy was found to be dented and stained, with its base hanging off, after Europe's exciting victory over the USA at Valderrama in 1997. Last seen at the post-match party, where it was handed around as players drank champagne from it, the Cup was returned to its spiritual home of the Belfry in Sutton Coldfield, home to the British PGA. But instead of being sent straight to a bank vault, it was transported by security company Securicor to a jeweller in nearby Birmingham to be repaired.

"The word is that it was dropped at the post-match party," said the goldsmith entrusted with the job of returning it to its former glory. Facing a bill of a few hundred pounds, a PGA spokesman admitted: "The cup was damaged during the celebrations. We are not saying a golfer dropped it, but the base was coming away and a dent needed repairing."

7 Just Call me Mystic Todd

As the World's leading professionals gathered in St Andrews in 2005 to compete for the Open, defending champ Todd Hamilton could have been forgiven if the first thing he did on arriving was seek out a local soothsayer!

He was a shock winner at Royal Troon the year before, when he overturned pre-tournament odds of 850–1 to beat Ernie Els in a dramatic four-hole play-off, but to hear him speak, the result was already written in the stars. A few months earlier, in March 2004, he had played in a pro-am at the Honda Classic with three amateurs, who told him that he was definitely going to win at Royal Troon!

How did they know? Well, it seems they had partnered Ben Curtis exactly a year before at the same event, and correctly predicted that he would come good at Royal St George's in 2003. But it did not end there!

During final practice over the Ayrshire course, Hamilton noticed his name was placed at the top of the leaderboard above the main grandstand by students running practice drills before the big off. Too good a chance to miss, he borrowed a friend's camera and took a few snaps for posterity.

"I know the guys working the scoreboard were practising putting up different names," said Hamilton later, "but I said to my caddie how cool it would be if my name was still up there on Sunday afternoon." Revealing a talent rivalling that of Mystic Meg, four days later it was, as he accepted the Silver Claret jug from the hand of HRH Prince Andrew.

8

To get ahead in golf, it helps to have a snappy name like 'Tiger' Woods, 'Jumbo' Ozaki or the 'Great White Shark.' So when it came to naming pro tournaments in the past, something definitely went wrong – like the Iron Lung Classic, last played in Atlanta, Georgia in the early 1950s for example. Other American tournaments with unusual names are the Rubber City Open, played in the mid-1960s, and The Hardscrabble Open played in the late 1940s.

It's not just a phenomenon of the past – in South Africa, they have the Cock o' the North tournament, and from Japan we have the DyDo-Drinco Shizuoka Open. As for a real mouthful we return to the European Seniors Tour, and the STC Bovis Lend Lease European Invitational.

9  Back to the Future

Ever wanted to predict the future? Perhaps make a killing on the Stock Exchange, or invent a golf club that would revolutionise the game? Way back in 1892, a remarkable book entitled *'Golf in the Year 2000'* was published by British author, John McCullough, in which he accurately predicted how golf would be played in the modern era.

Based on the adventures of a fanatical golfer named Alexander Gibson, this fascinating tale tells how he fell into a coma, only to wake up over a century later. Understandably, the world had changed beyond recognition except for two things – golf was still a popular pastime and St Andrews was still its spiritual home. Outlining an incredible vision of the future, it predicts, amongst other things, metal-headed woods, electric golf buggies, and even live televised golf from America! All this in the bygone days of wooden-shafted clubs and gutta-percha balls!

10  Will the Real Tiger Stand Up

In 2001, Tiger Woods gave evidence at the trial of a 31-year-old man who was accused of impersonating him. Using his real name of Eldrick T. Woods to run up a $17,000 credit card debt, the perpetrator somehow obtained Woods' social security number, and a fake driver's licence in his name. Hearing the case at a courthouse in Sacramento, California, a storage locker rented in Woods' name was also found, stuffed with electrical goods and other items.

Not surprisingly, the superstar golfer denied renting the locker, or purchasing the items found inside. During his evidence, the golfer was asked about a used luxury car bought in his name. "It's not a Buick!" he said in mock surprise, referring to one of his multi-million-dollar sponsorship deals with one of America's best-known motor companies. Woods then explained how he usually pays cash for everything and hated shopping, as he would 'rather go and play (golf).'

Almost made the cut

A BUZZ OF EXCITEMENT

In 1966, the year England beat Germany to win the World Cup at Wembley, Gary Player and Jack Nicklaus had a match of their own at Zwartkop in South Africa. Attacked by a huge swarm of bees, they covered their heads with towels and made a run for it before wisely settling for a half on the hole. What they did not know is that African wild bees kill more people each year than any other form of wildlife!

CUSTOM FIT

Golf is full of tradition, especially in Scotland. One of the most venerable concerns parading a full-size silver club through the streets of St. Andrews before the installation of a new club captain. Tradition also requires the incoming captain to attach a silver golf ball to the shaft (gold if royal) in memory of bygone times. Curiously, he is then asked to kiss the silver club as a mark of respect, and this quaint ceremony is known as 'kissing the captain's balls!'

A GOOD CASE FOR DIVORCE

Chicago judge Joseph Sabath ruled in 1925 that, "golf widowhood is not yet grounds for divorce" even though "the husband is a hopeless duffer with a wretched drive, who spends most of his time on the golf course."

Selected Bibliography

Braid, James. Advanced Golf, *Methuen, London, 1908*.

Browning, Robert K. A History of Golf. *London: J. M. Dent, 1955*.

Campbell, Patrick. How to Become a Scratch Golfer. *Anthony Blond, 1963*.

Clark, Robert. Golf: A Royal & Ancient Game, *Edinburgh, 1875*.

Dalconen, A. J. Golf: The History of the Royal & Ancient Game, *Salamander, 1995*.

Fitzpatrick, H. L. Golf Don'ts. *Doubleday – Page, 1900*.

Fletcher, Charles. How to Play Bad Golf. *Los Angeles: privately printed, 1935*.

Golf Monthly, *IPC Publications, Stamford Street, London*.

Golf World magazine (UK), *EMAP Active, Peterborough.*

Golf Illustrated/Golf Weekly, *EMAP Active, Peterborough.*

Harris, Robert. Sixty Years of Golf, *Batchworth Press, 1953.*

Hanks, Charles Stedman. Hints to Golfers, *NY: Salem Press, 1903.*

Hutchinson, Horace *et al.* Golf: Longmans Green, *London, 1890.*

Hutchinson, Horace. Fifty Years of Golf, *Country Life, 1919.*

Hyslop, Theodore. Mental Handicaps in Golf, *Tindall & Cox, 1927.*

Keeler, O. B. The Bobby Jones Story. *Tupper and Love, Atlanta, 1959.*

Kenneth R. The Mental Side of Golf: A Study of the Game, *Muller, 1955.*

Kerr. J. The Golf Book of East Lothian, *Constable, Edinburgh, 1896.*

MacKenzie, Alister. Golf Course Architecture. *Simpkin, Marshall, Hamilton and Kent, London, 1920.*

Mappin, Major G. F. The Golfing You, *Skeffington, 1948.*

185

Ouimet, Francis. A Game Of Golf. The Francis Ouimet Scholarship Fund Inc. Weston, *Mass. USA.*

Park, William. The Game of Golf, *Longmans, 1899.*

Potter, Stephen. Golfmanship, © *Stephen Potter, 1968.*

Price, Charles, ed. *The American Golfer magazine.*

Rice, Grantland, *The American Golfer magazine.*

Robertson, James K. St.Andrews. Fife, *Scot.: Citizen Office, 1967.*

Simpson, Sir Walter. The Art of Golf, *Hamilton. Edinburgh, 1887.*

Sneddon, Richard, The Golf Stream, *Philadelphia, Dorrance, 1941.*

Veteran, A. The Secret of Golf for Occasional Players, *L: Methuen 1922.*

Wind, Herbert W. The Story of American Golf. *New York: Farrar, Straus, 1948.*

Wind, Herbert Warren, ed. The Complete Golfer. *New York: Simon and Schuster, 1954.*

Wethered, Roger & Joyce. Golf from Two Sides: *Longmans, 1922.*